JUDAICA

A SHORT-TITLE CATALOGUE OF THE BOOKS, PAMPHLETS AND
MANUSCRIPTS RELATING TO THE POLITICAL, SOCIAL AND CULTURAL
HISTORY OF THE JEWS AND TO THE JEWISH QUESTION

In the Library of

LUDWIG ROSENBERGER

Chicago, Illinois

EXPANDED SUPPLEMENT

CINCINNATI

HEBREW UNION COLLEGE PRESS

1979

This expanded supplement completely replaces the
supplement published in 1974. All items added to the
Rosenberger Collection since 1974 are interfiled, in
this expanded supplement, with the items added
before 1974 but after publication of the basic volume
in 1971.

Special thanks are due to Ms. Vera Sanker,
Ms. Andrea Solomon and Ms. Sue Teller for
copy-editing and proof-reading.

H.C.Z.

BIBLIOGRAPHICA JUDAICA 4 (revised)

A bibliographic series of The Library of Hebrew Union College –
Jewish Institute of Religion
Edited by Herbert C. Zafren, Professor of Jewish Bibliography
Hebrew Union College – Jewish Institute of Religion

DICTIONARIES

Who's Who in World Jewry. A Biographical Dictionary of Outstanding Jews. New York, etc., 1972.

PERIODICALS

Das Jüdische Magazin. Volume 1, number 1–4. Berlin, 1929. *Complete run.*

Schlemiel. Illustriertes jüdisches Witzblatt. (Editor, Max Jungmann.) Volume 1, number 1–2; volume 2, number 1–3. Berlin, 1903–1904. *Complete run?*

BIBLIOGRAPHY

ALTSHULER, MORDECHAI (editor) Russian Publications on Jews and Judaism in the Soviet Union 1917–1967. Jerusalem, 1970.

BERLIN, CHARLES (editor) Hebrew Manuscripts in the Houghton Library of the Harvard College Library. A Catalogue . . . Cambridge, Massachusetts, 1975.

BERLIN, CHARLES. Library Resources for Jewish Studies in the United States. Cambridge, Massachusetts, 1975.

BRISMAN, SHIMEON. A History and Guide to Judaic Bibliography. Cincinnati and New York, 1977.

[*Dresden*] Katalog der Bücherei der Israelitischen Religionsgemeinde zu Dresden (Dresden) 1927.

[*Dreyfus*] LISPSCHUTZ, LÉON [recte: LIPSCHUTZ] Une bibliothèque dreyfusienne. Essai de Bibliographie thématique et analytique de l'affaire Dreyfus. Paris, 1970.

FÜRSTENBERG, HANS. Napoleon als Büchersammler. Illustriert durch Beispiele aus der Sammlung des Verfassers. Berlin, 1931.

GOLB, NORMAN. Spertus College of Judaica Yemenite Manuscripts. An Illustrated Catalogue. Chicago, 1972.

Harvard University Library. Widener Library Shelflist 39. Judaica. Cambridge, Massachusetts, 1971.

Harvard University Library. Judaica in the Houghton Library. Cambridge, Massachusetts, 1972.

[*Heine*] SEIFERT, SIEGFRIED (editor) Heine-Bibliographie 1954–1964. Berlin and Weimar, 1968.

Jewish Book Annual. Volume 35 (5738/1977–1978) New York, 1977.

The Jewish People and Palestine. A Bibliophilic Pilgrimage Through Five Centuries. Cambridge, Massachusetts, 1973. *Exhibition catalogue at Harvard.*

KAGANOFF, NATHAN M. Supplement III: Judaica Americana printed before 1851. New York, 1971. *Offprint.*

[*Kiev, I. Edward*] Studies in Jewish Bibliography, History and Literature in honor of I. Edward Kiev (editor, Charles Berlin). New York, 1971.

[*Landau*] Catalogue of very important Illuminated Manuscripts and Printed Books selected from the renowned library formed by Baron Horace de Landau (1824–1903) . . . London, 1948. *Sales catalogue.*

Liste der für Jugendliche und Büchereien ungeeigneten Druckschriften. Herausgegeben vom Reichsministerium für Volksaufklärung und Propaganda Abteilung Schrifttum. Leipzig, 1940. *First edition.*

[*Luzzatti, Luigi*] Catalogo della Biblioteca "Luigi Luzzatti" (Roma) 1924.

[*Poch, Bernardo*] Del Pentateuco stampato in Napoli l'anno MCCCCXCI e saggio di alcune varianti lezioni estratte da esso e da'libri antichi della sinagoga. Roma, 1780.

RABINOWICZ, HARRY M. Treasures of Judaica. South Brunswick, etc., 1971.

[*Regenstein Library*] A Catalogue to an Exhibition of Notable Books and Manuscripts from the Collections of The University of Chicago Library Prepared for the Dedication of The Joseph Regenstein Library . . . 1970 (Chicago, 1970)

[*Schocken*] Die Bibliotheken Salman Schocken-Karl Wolfskehl. 2 volumes. Hamburg, 1975, 1976. *Auction catalogue.*

SHMERUK, KH. (editor) Jewish Publications in the Soviet Union 1917–1960. Jerusalem, 1961.

[*Wiener Library*] Prejudice. Racist – Religious – Nationalist. Catalogue Series number 5. London, 1971.

WOLFSON, HARRY A. Hebrew Books in Harvard. Cambridge, Massachusetts, 1968. *Offprint.*

AUTOGRAPH LETTERS

BEN GURION, D. Autograph Letter Signed, 1 page. Sdeh Boker, September 30, 1963. To group of students at Matawan Regional High School, Matawan, New Jersey.

BENDAVID, L[AZARUS] Autograph Letter Signed, 1 page. Berlin, November 16 [18]15. Attests that the boys Samuel Is. Seemann and Wolf Lesser attend the Jüdische Freischule and are as worthy as needy of support.

BRANDES, GEORGE. Autograph Letter Signed, 1 page. Copenhagen, December 9 [18]95. To unknown addressee concerning sale of his book in America.

[*Disraeli*] Letter in unknown hand on Lord Beaconsfield's own mourning stationery concerning his funeral. "Her Majesty desires wishes in Lord Beaconsfield's will to be strictly observed."

D'ISRAELI [ISAAC] Autograph Letter, 1 page. Written in the third person, dated June 5th, no year, to Mr. Dubois.

FRIEDRICH [II., KING OF PRUSSIA] Letter Signed, 3 pages. Potsdam, July 4th, 1752. To Oberst von Retzow concerning the privileges granted to the Schutz-Jude Hertz Mohses Gumpertz and the commercial activities of the Jews in general.

FRIEDRICH [II., KING OF PRUSSIA] Letter Signed, 2 pages. Potsdam, August 29, 1753. To Oberst von Retzow forbidding Jews to be in the "Campement bey Spandau" nor any commercial activities of Jews there.

GOMPERS, SAM[UEL] Letter Signed, 1 page. Washington, District of Columbia, March 31, 1899. To Hamilton Holt [editor, *The Independent*] New York.

[*Mendelssohn, Dorothea*] SCHLEGEL, DOROTHEA VON. Autograph Letter Signed, 1½ pages [Frankfurt am Main] December 27 [18]31. To Elisabeth Malss, sending wine out of Christian religious motivations. Additional note, 1½ pages. No dates. Mentioning her son Philipp [Veit] *See Stargardt Katalog 599.*

TROTSKY, L. Letter Signed, 1 page. Büyükada, January 6, 1931. To Herr Boni concerning arrangements for the publication of his "History of the Russian Revolution."

WOLF, SIMON. Letter Signed, 1 page. Washington, District of Columbia, October 24, 1918. To Press Association Compilers, Inc., New York, concerning his German provenance.

INCUNABULA

Biblia Latina. Venice, Nicolaus Jenson, 1479. *Hain, 3073.*

ALMANACHS

FEIWEL, BERTHOLD (editor) Juedischer Almanach 5663. Berlin [1903]

THIEBERGER, FRIEDRICH AND WELTSCH, FELIX (editors) Jüdischer Almanach auf das Jahr 5688. Prag (1927)

Almanach des Schocken Verlags auf das Jahr 5694. Berlin, 1933/34.

CALENDARS

ABELES, OTTO AND BATÓ, LUDWIG (editors) Jüdischer Nationalkalender Almanach auf das Jahr 5682 (1921–1922) Wien, 1921.

BUCHNER, J. K. Jahrbuch für Israeliten auf das Jahr der Welt 5625–1865. Zweite Folge. Leipzig (1864)

Das Jahr 1938. Kalender der Berliner Juden (Berlin, 1937)

Kalender und Jahrbuch für Israeliten auf das Jahr 5603. Wien, 1842.

LIEBERMANN, H. (editor) Deutscher Volks-Kalender [und Jahrbuch] Insbesondere zum Gebrauch für Israeliten auf das Jahr 1857, 1882, 1883. Brieg. *Each volume bound together with "Jahrbuch."*

WERTHEIM, PH. (editor) Kalender und Jahrbuch auf das Jahr 5618 für die jüdischen Gemeinden Preussens. Berlin, 1858.

WERTHEIMER, JOSEF (editor) Jahrbuch für Israeliten 5616 (1855–1856) Wien, 1855.

ART

BARAMKI, DIMITRI C. The Art and Architecture of Ancient Palestine. Beirut, Lebanon, 1969.

BERENSON, BERNHARD. Die Florentinischen Maler der Renaissance. Oppeln, Leipzig, 1898.

BERENSON, BERNARD. The Passionate Sightseer. From the diaries 1947 to 1956. New York, 1960.

[*Berenson*] ALEXANDER, FRANCES AND SIDNEY (editors) The Berenson Collection. Milano, 1964.

[*Bernhardt*] BARING, MAURICE. Sarah Bernhardt (London) 1933.

BERNHARDT, LYSIANE. Sarah Bernhardt ma grand'mère. Paris, 1947.

[*Bernhardt*] (BERTON, PIERRE) The Real Sarah Bernhardt Whom Her Audiences Never Knew, Told to Her Friend Mme. Pierre Berton . . . New York, 1924.

[*Bernhardt*] SKINNER, CORNELIA OTIS. Madame Sarah. Boston, 1967.

[*Cummings*] Major Works from the Collection of Nathan Cummings. Chigaco, 1973.

DAVIDOVICZ, DAVID. Wandmalereien in alten Synagogen. Das Wirken des Malers Elieser Sussmann in Deutschland. Hameln-Hannover, 1969.

FRIEDENBERG, DANIEL M. Jewish Minters and Medalists. Philadelphia, 1976.

[*Israels, Jozef*] STAHL, FRITZ. Josef Israels. Berlin, 1903.

KAYSER, STEPHEN S. AND SCHOENBERGER, GUIDO (editors) Jewish Ceremonial Art. Philadelphia, 1959.

LONDON, HANNAH R. Shades of My Forefathers. Springfield, Massachusetts, 1941. *Limited signed edition.*

[*Loutchansky*] LEVINSON, ANDRÉ. Jacques Loutchansky (Les artistes Juifs) Paris, no date.

MAYER, AUGUST L. Geschichte der spanischen Malerei. 2 volumes. Leipzig, 1913.

MAYER, AUGUST L. Gotik in Spanien. Leipzig, 1928.

MAYER, AUGUST L. El Greco. Berlin, 1931.

MAYER, AUG. L. (editor) Expressionistische Miniaturen des deutschen Mittelalters. München, 1918.

MAYER, AUGUST L. Mittelalterliche Plastik in Italien. München, 1923.

MAYER, AUGUST L. Mittelalterliche Plastik in Spanien. München, 1922.

MAYER, AUGUST L. Die Sevillaner Malerschule. Beiträge zu ihrer Geschichte. Leipzig, 1911.

MENGS, ANTONIO RAFFAELE. Le più belle teste del celebre a fresco delle Stanze Vaticane comunemente denominato a scuola di Atene dipinte da Raffaele d'Urbino disegnate da A.R.M. incise da Domenico Cunego [Roma, 1783] *Drawn by Mengs, engraved by Cunego.*

MODIGLIANI [AMADEO] Peintures (Editor, San Lazzaro) Paris, 1947.

(*Modigliani*) Fusero, Clemente. Il romanzo di Modigliani (Milano, 1957)

[*Myers*] ROSENBAUM, JEANETTE W. Myer Myers, Goldsmith 1723-1795. Philadelphia, 1954.

NAMENYI, ERNEST. The Essence of Jewish Art. New York and London, 1960.

[*Reinhardt, Max*] SAYLER, OLIVER M. (editor) Max Reinhardt and his Theatre. New York, 1924.

SAULCY, F. DE. Histoire de l'art judaïque tirée des textes sacrés et profanes. Paris, 1864.

SCHWEITZER, ETIENNE. La colonne en spirale image de la vie. Metz, 1963.

[*Shahn, Ben*] PRESCOTT, KENNETH W. Ben Shahn: A Retrospective 1898-1969. New York, 1977.

[*Steinhardt*] PFEFFERKORN, RUDOLF. Jakob Steinhardt. Berlin, 1967.

STRAUSS, HEINRICH. Die Kunst der Juden im Wandel der Zeit und Umwelt. Das Judenproblem im Spiegel der Kunst. Tübingen, 1972.

ART: MAX LIEBERMANN

Max Liebermann 1847-1935. Ausstellung 1954 Kunsthalle Bremen (Bremen, 1954)

GOLDSCHMIDT, ADOLPH. Gedenkrede auf Max Liebermann 1935 (Hamburg) 1954.

HEINE, HEINRICH. Der Rabbi von Bacherach. Mit Originallithographien von Max Liebermann. Berlin, 1923. *Limited, numbered, signed edition.*

LICHTWARK, ALFRED. Briefe an Max Liebermann. Hamburg, 1947.

EXHIBITION AND AUCTION CATALOGUES

American Jewish Art Club. Golden Anniversary at Spertus Museum. Chicago, 1978. *Exhibition catalogue.*

American Jewish Ephemera. A Bicentennial Exhibition from the Judaica Collection of the Harvard College Library. Cambridge, Massachusetts, 1977.

Bericht über die Gründungsversammlung des Jüdischen Museumsvereins Berlin (Berlin, 1929)

[*Berlin*] Leistung und Schicksal. 300 Jahre Jüdische Gemeinde zu Berlin. Ausstellung . . . 1971. Berlin, 1971. *Catalogue.*

[*Breslau*] Verein Jüdisches Museum E. V. zu Breslau (Breslau) no date.

[*Fenster*] Judaic Treasures from the . . . Fenster Gallery of Jewish Art, Tulsa, Oklahoma (Tulsa) 1973.

(*Goldschmidt-Przibram*) Collection Goldschmidt-Przibram de Bruxelles. Catalogue . . . Amsterdam, 1924. *Auction catalogue.*

[*Hirsch*] The Robert von Hirsch Collection. 4 volumes (London) 1978. *Auction catalogue.*

[*Huldschinsky*] Sammlung Oscar Huldschinsky Berlin. Voranzeige. Berlin, 1928. *Auction catalogue.*

Important Hebrew Books. Sotheby Parke-Bernet. New York, 1972. *Auction catalogue.*

Israël à travers les âges. Paris, 1968. *Exhibition catalogue.*

Judaica . . . Parke-Bernet, New York, 1971. *Auction catalogue.*

Judaica. New York, 1976. *Auction catalogue of Sotheby Parke-Bernet.*

Judaica and Other Works of Art. New York, 1978. *Auction catalogue of Sotheby Parke-Bernet.*

[*Kafka*] Franz Kafka 1883–1924. An Exhibition . . . Berlin (1968) *Catalogue.*

[*Karp*] Some Books of the People of the Book. An Exhibit . . . from the collection of Abraham J. Karp . . . 1971. Rochester, New York (1972)

[*Levine*] The Rubin Levine Collection of Judaica. New York, 1974. *Auction catalogue.*

[*Lewisohn, Adolph*] The Adolph Lewisohn Collection of Modern French Paintings and Sculptures . . . New York, 1928.

[*Loewenthal*] Sammlung Ludwig Loewenthal Berlin. Berlin, 1931. *Auction catalogue.*

Magic and Superstition in the Jewish Tradition. Chicago, 1975. *Exhibition catalogue.*

[*Meidner*] Ludwig Meidner. Recklinghausen, etc., 1963. *Exhibition catalogue.*

[*Mendelssohn-Bartholdy*] Felix Mendelssohn Bartholdy. Bodleian Library, Oxford, 1972. *Exhibition catalogue.*

[*Mendelssohn-Bartholdy*] Felix Mendelssohn Bartholdy. Dokumente seines Lebens. Ausstellung zum 125. Todestag . . . Berlin-Dahlem, 1972. *Exhibition catalogue.*

[*Modigliani*] RUSSOLI, FRANCO (editor) Mostra di Amedeo Modigliani. Milano, 1958.

[*Mosse*] Kunstsammlung Rudolf Mosse, Berlin. Berlin, 1934. *Auction catalogue.*

[*Oppenheim, Albert*] Collection Baron Albert Oppenheim Cöln. 2 volumes. Berlin and München, 1914. *Auction catalogue.*

[*Prague*] Kunstschätze. Staatliches Jüdisches Museum Prag. Wien, 1970. *Exhibition catalogue.*

[*Regenstein*] The Helen and Ruth Regenstein Collection of Rare Books. A Selection Exhibited at the . . . University of Chicago. Chicago, 1975.

(*Rosenfeld-Goldschmidt*) Catalogue de la Collection Rosenfeld-Goldschmidt. 2 volumes. Amsterdam, 1916. *Auction catalogue.*

[*Rothenstein*] Catalogue of an Exhibition of Paintings, Drawings, and Lithographs by William Rothenstein. New York, 1911.

[*Sachs*] Sammlung Carl Sachs. Internationale Graphik des XIX. Jahrhunderts . . . Leipzig and Berlin, 1931. *Auction catalogue.*

[*Sassoon*] Catalogue of the Sassoon Collection of highly important Hebrew Printed Books. 2 volumes. London, 1970–1971. *Auction catalogue.*

[*Schwadron*] Catalogue of the Exhibition of Autographs and Portraits of Famous Jews from the Collection Dr. Abraham Schwadron. Jerusalem, 1927. *Hebrew.*

[*Seligmann*] Sammlung Kommerzienrat M. Seligmann† Köln a.Rh. München, 1917. *Auction catalogue.*

[*Seligsohn*] Die Sammlung Richard Seligsohn. Ostasiatische Kunst. Berlin, 1926.

[*Spertus*] The Maurice Spertus Museum of Judaica. An Illustrated Catalog of Selected Objects. Chicago, 1974.

STEIN, GÜNTER. Die Judaica des Historischen Museums der Pfalz. Speyer, 1969. *Offprint.*

A Walk Through the Past (Hebrew Union College Skirball Museum) Los Angeles, 1974. *Exhibition catalogue.*

DRAMAS AND POETRY

CUMBERLAND, RICHARD. Der Jude. Ein Schauspiel in fünf Aufzügen. Leipzig, no date.

CUMBERLAND, RICHARD. Der Jude. Ein Schauspiel in fünf Aufzügen. Leipzig (Reclam) no date.

[*Falkensohn, Issachar Behr*] Gedichte von einem pohlnischen Juden. Mietau and Leipzig, 1772.

[*Falkensohn, Issachar Behr*] Anhang zu den Gedichten eines pohlnischen Juden. Mietau and Leipzig, 1772.

HAUSHOFER, MAX. Der ewige Jude. Ein dramatisches Gedicht in drei Theilen. Leipzig, 1894.

WEIS, KARL. Der polnische Jude. Volksoper in 2 Acten. Text . . . von Victor Léon und Richard Batka. Leipzig, no date.

MISCELLANEOUS AUTHORS AND BIOGRAPHIES

HERTZKA, THEODOR. Das soziale Problem. Berlin, 1912.

KAHLER, ERICH. The Rallying Idea. Santa Barbara, 1967.

KOHN, HANS. Bürger vieler Welten. Ein Leben im Zeitalter der Weltrevolution. Frauenfeld, 1965.

LASKER, EMANUEL. Die Selbsttäuschungen unserer Feinde. Berlin, no date.

[*Ricardo*] SOTIROFF, G. Ricardo und Sismondi. Zürich and New York, 1945.

[*Rosenblum*] SANT'ANA DIONISIO, JOSÉ. Salomon Rosenblum. Biografia e obra cientifica. Paris, 1960.

VELIKOVSKY, IMMANUEL. Worlds in Collision. New York, 1950.

FICTION

JACOBOWSKI, LUDWIG. Werther, der Jude. Roman. Berlin, no date.

JUSCHKEWITSCH, S. Die Parias. Erzählung aus dem Leben der russischen Juden. München, no date.

BALLIN, GÜNTHER. Zwischen gestern und morgen. Buenos Aires, 1945.

LEVI, CARLO. La doppia notte dei tigli. No place, 1959.

LOEWENBERG, JAKOB. Aus zwei Quellen. Die Geschichte eines deutschen Juden. Berlin, 1919.

STERNER, LAWRENCE. The Un-Christian Jew. New York, 1919.

GENERAL JUDAICA I, *to 1850*

Altercatio Synagogae et Ecclesiae, in qua bona omnium fere utriusque Instrumenti librorum pars explicatur: opus peruetustum ac insigne. Coloniae, 1540.

[BOYER D'ARGENS, JEAN-BAPTISTE] Mémoires du Comte de Vaxère, ou le faux Rabin, par l'Auteur des Lettres Juives. Amsterdam, 1737.

BÜSING, JOHANNES CHRISTOPHORUS. Dissertatio theologico-philologica de tubis Hebraeorum argenteis . . . Bremae, 1745.

BUXTORF, JOHANNES. Epitome radicum hebraicarum et chaldaicarum complectens . . . Basileae, 1607.

BYTHNER, VICTORINUS. . . . Lingua eruditorum; sive methodica institutio linguae sanctae . . . Londini, 1675. *Roth, B15/6.*

CELLARIUS, CHRISTOPHORUS. Grammatica Ebraea in tabulis synopticis . . . Cizae, 1684.

CURTIUS, SEBASTIANUS. Radices linguae sanctae Hebraeae . . . Geismariae, 1649.

DANZ, JOH. ANDREAS. Antiquitas baptismi initiationis Israelitarum vindicata, contra adscribentes ipsi originem Christianam. Jenae, 1710.

DANZ, J. A. Interpres Ebraeo-Chaldaeus . . . Jenae, 1715.

DANZ, J. A. Manuductio, viam ostendens compendiosam ad Ebraeae Linguae analysin faciliùs instituendam, . . . Jenae, 1702.

DANZ, J. A. Paradigmata nominum simplicium . . . Jenae, 1709.

DRUSIUS, IOH. De sectis Iudaicis commentarii . . . (editor, Josephus Scaliger) Arnhemiae, 1619.

EBER, PAUL. L'estat de la religion et republique du peuple Iudaique, Depuis le retour de l'exil de Babylone iusques au dernier saccagement de Ierusalem. Lyon, 1564.

FECHTIUS, JOHANNES. Disquisitio de Judaica ecclesia . . . Argentorati, 1630. *Dissertation.*

FLEURY [CLAUDE] Les mœurs des Israélites. Paris, 1683.

FLEURY [CLAUDE] Les mœurs des Israélites, . . . Bruxelles, 1753.

FLEURI [sic] [CLAUDE] Mœurs des Israelites. Louvain, 1773. *Bound with: Moeurs des Chrétiens, Louvain, 1773.*

FLEURY [CLAUDE] Mœurs des Israélites et des Chrétiens. Tours, 1804.

FLEURY [CLAUDE] Mœurs des Israélites et des Chrétiens. Paris, 1808.

FLEURY [CLAUDE] Mœurs des Israélites et des Chrétiens. Lille, 1821.

FLEURY [CLAUDE] Mœurs des Israélites et des Chrétiens. Tours, 1836.

FLEURY [CLAUDE] Mœurs des Israélites et des Chrétiens. Tours, 1842.

FLEURY [CLAUDE] Mœurs des Israélites et des Chrétiens. Tours, 1844.

FLEURY [CLAUDE] Costumi degl'Israeliti . . . Venezia, 1712. *Two parts in one volume. Parte seconda: Costumi de' Cristiani.*

FLEURY, [CLAUDE] Costumi degl' Israeliti . . . Venezia, 1755. *Two parts in one volume. Parte seconda: Costumi de' Cristiani.*

FLEURY [CLAUDE] Costumi degl'Israeliti . . . Venezia, 1789. *Two parts in one volume. Parte seconda: Costumi dei Cristiani.*

FLEURI [CLAUDE] De zeeden der Israeliten . . . (editor D. Ghys) Amsterdam, 1715.

FLEURI, CLAUDIO. Las costumbres de los Israelitas, . . . Barcelona, 1769.

FLEURY [CLAUDE] Os costumes dos Israelitas, . . . Lisboa, 1778.

FLEURY [CLAUDE] Obyczaie Izraelitow. Roku, 1783.

GAUDELIUS, JOHANNES PHILIPPUS. Beth Hamidrash sive Antiquitates Academicae . . . Hanoviae, 1703.

GUARIN, PETRUS. Grammatica hebraica et chaldaica . . . 2 volumes. Lutetiae Parisiorum, 1724–1726.

GUARIN, PETRUS. Lexicon hebraicum et chaldaeo-biblicum . . . Lutetiae Parisiorum, 1746.

HEMPEL, ERNESTUS GUILIELMUS. Prima linguae ebraicae elementa . . . Lipsiae, 1789.

IKENIUS, CONRADUS. Dissertatio theologico-philologica de finibus terrae promissae hujusque successiva occupatione . . . Bremae, 1745.

KLIPSTEIN, IACOBUS CHRISTIANUS. De autonomia Iudaeorum, commentatio academica. Gissae, 1739. *Dissertation. Freimann, page 368.*

L'EMPEREUR, CONSTANTIN (editor) D. Isaaci Abrabanielis & R. Mosis Alschechi Comment. in Esaiae Prophetiam 30 . . . Lugduni Batavorum (Elzevir) 1631.

LEUSDEN, JOHANNES. Philologus Hebraeo-Graecus Generalis, continens Quaestiones Hebraeo-Graecas, Quae circa Novum Testamentum Graecum fere moveri solent. Ultrajecti, 1670.

[LIGHTFOOTE, JOHANNES] Horae Hebraicae et Talmudicae, impensae in Evangelium S. Johannis. Londini, 1671. *Bound with another volume, not catalogued.*

LIMBORCH, PHILIPPUS A. De veritate religionis Christianae amica collatio cum erudito Judaeo. Basileae, 1740.

LOSIUS, JOH. JUSTUS. Discursus theologico philologicus de successiva corruptione Judaeorum, . . . Wernigerodae [about 1710]

MEZGER, P. F. CASIMIRUS. Poesis Hebraica, publicae disputationi submissa . . . Romae, 1774. *Dissertation.*

MEZGER, PAULUS. Sacra historia de gentis hebraicae ortu . . . Augustae Vindelicorum and Dilingae, 1700.

NEANDER, MICHAEL. Sanctae linguae Hebraeae Erotemata . . . Basileae, 1567.

PARREIDT, IO. HENRICUS AND WINCKLERUS, CAROLUS GODOFREDUS. De auro Iudaico. Lipsiae [1743]

PASINI, JOSEPHUS. . . . Grammatica linguae sanctae institutio, cum vocum omnium anomalarum indice, et explicatione. Patavii, 1766.

PFEIFFER, AUGUSTUS. . . . Dissertatio philologica de Targumim . . . Wittebergae, 1665.

PFEIFFER, AUGUSTUS. Fasciculus dissertationum philologicarum, . . . de Talmude Judaeorum . . . Wittebergae, 1665.

PFEIFFER, AUGUSTUS. Tractatus philologico-antirabbinicus . . . Wittebergae, 1666.

RAABIUS, CHRISTOPHORUS THEOPHILUS. Dissertatio theologica de mysterio conversionis Iudaicae gentis ante mundi finem . . . Giessae, 1716.

REUSCHIUS, IOHANNES PETRUS. De naturali fundamento linguae Ebraeorum . . . Ienae, 1718.

[*Sabatai Zevi*] Wahre Beschreibung Des Neuen Propheten, So sich in diesem 1687. Jahre zu Alkair in Egypten sehen lässet. Nebst einer kurtzen Beschreibung seiner Lehre, Lebens und Wandels. No place, no date.

[*Sabatai Zevi*] Die Geschichte von dem grossen Betrieger oder falschen Juden Könige Sabatai-Sevi von Smirna . . . [Cöthen] 1702. *Edition with three large copper-plates.*

[SCHICKARD, WILHELM] Horologium Hebraeum, sive consilium . . . Lipsiae, 1624.

SCHICKARD, WILHELM. Horologium Hebraeum sive consilium . . . Lipsiae, 1659.

SCHROEDER, NIC. GUIL. Institutiones ad fundamenta linguae Hebraeae in usum studiosae juventutis. Claudiopoli, 1772.

SIGONIUS, CAROLUS. De rep. Hebraeorum libri VII . . . Coloniae, 1583.

STEINERSDORFF, JOHANN CHRISTIAN. Hebräische Grammatik . . . Halle, 1767.

SURENHUSIUS, GUILIELMUS. Sepher hamashveh . . . in quo secundum veterum theologorum Hebraeorum formulas allegandi . . . Amstelaedami, 1713.

VIO, THOMAS DE. Parabolae Salomonis ad Veritatem Hebraicam Castigatae . . . Lugduni, 1545.

WALTHER, CHRISTOPHORUS THEODOSIUS. Ellipses Hebraicae, sive de vocibus . . . Dresdae et Lipsiae, 1740.

WEITENAUER, IGNATIUS. Trifolium Chaldaicum, sive nova grammaticae methodus . . . Augustae Vindelicorum and Friburgi Brisgoiae, 1759.

WEITENAUER, IGNATIUS. Trifolium Hebraicum sive nova grammaticae biblicae methodus . . . Augustae Vindelicorum and Oeniponti, 1756.

WEITENAUER, IGNATIUS. Trifolium Hebraicum, sive nova grammaticae biblicae methodus . . . Augustae Vindelicorum and Friburgi Brisgoiae, 1759.

WEITENAUER, IGNATIUS. Trifolium Syriacum, sive nova grammaticae methodus . . . Augustae Vindelicorum and Friburgi Brisgoiae, 1759.

WIDENHOFER, FRANCISCUS XAV. Rudimenta Hebraica paucis ad linguam sacram facile addiscendam comprehensa . . . Wirceburgi, 1747.

WOLFFIUS, CHRISTIAN. GOTTL. FRIDERICUS. Schediasma philologicum de divortio Judaeorum . . . Lipsiae, 1739.

ZENDRINI, ANGELO. Riflessioni sopra l'Origine della Lingua Ebraica (Padova, 1785)

GENERAL JUDAICA II, *from 1851*

Allgemeine Jüdische Kolonisations-Organisation (Berlin) no date. *Prospectus.*

ALTMANN, A. (editor) Between East and West. Essays Dedicated to the Memory of Bela Horovitz. London, 1958.

BAECK, LEO. Two Series of Lectures . . . (New York, 1950)

BARDET, JEAN-GASTON. Le trséor secret d'Ishraël [*sic*] Paris, 1970.

BERL, HEINRICH. Das Judentum in der Musik. Berlin and Leipzig, 1926.

BLOCH, JOSEPH S. Israel und die Völker. Nach jüdischer Lehre. Berlin and Wien, 1922.

Premier Congrès mondial de la jeunesse juive . . . 1958. Jérusalem, 1959.

FACKENHEIM, EMIL L. The Human Condition after Auschwitz. A Jewish Testimony a Generation after. Syracuse, 1971.

GHERCHENSON, MICHEL. Les destinées du peuple Juif. Paris, 1946.

GOLDMANN, FELIX. Warum sind und bleiben wir Juden? Berlin, 1924.

HEINEMANN, I. Zeitfragen im Lichte jüdischer Lebensanschauung. Frankfurt am Main, 1921.

IVRITH (pseudonym) The Jewish Character. No place, no date.

LAMPARTER, EDUARD. Das Judentum in seiner kultur- und religionsgeschichtlichen Erscheinung. Gotha, 1928.

LEWIN, ISAAC. Religious Jewry and the United Nations. Addresses before the United Nations. New York, 1953.

MONTEFIORE, CLAUDE G. Het Liberale Jodendom. Baarn, 1934.

NEWMAN, H. (editor) The Real Jew. Some Aspects of the Jewish Contribution to Civilization. London, 1925.

REINACH, THÉODORE. Juifs. Paris, 1894. *Extrait de la "Grande Encyclopédie."*

ROSTEN, LEO. The Joys of Yiddish. New York, etc., 1968.

ROTH, CECIL. Judah Abenzara's Map of the Mediterranean World, 1500 [Cincinnati] 1971.

SANDMEL, SAMUEL. After the Ghetto. Jews in Western Culture, Art, and Intellect. Syracuse, 1974.

SCHOEPS, HANS JOACHIM. Jüdische Geisteswelt. Zeugnisse aus zwei Jahrtausenden. Darmstadt and Genf, no date.

SCHOLEM, GERSHOM. Judaica. 2 volumes. Frankfurt am Main, 1963–1970.

[*Silveira*] GLASER, EDWARD. Miguel da Silveira's El Macabeo. No place, 1958.

VAN DEN HAAG, ERNEST. The Jewish Mystique. New York, 1971.

HISTORY

ABRAMSKY, C. War, Revolution and the Jewish Dilemma. London, 1975.

BRANN, M. Geschichte der Juden und ihrer Literatur. 3 volumes in 1. Breslau, 1910, 1911, 1913.

DUKER, ABRAHAM G. AND BEN-HORIN, MEIR (editors) Emancipation and Counter-Emancipation. Selected Essays from Jewish Social Studies (New York) 1974.

FISHMAN, JOSHUA A. (editor) Studies in Modern Jewish Social History. New York, 1972.

KASTEIN, JOSEF [pseudonym of JULIUS KATZENSTEIN] Een geschiedenis der Joden. Arnhem, 1933.

RIVKIN, ELLIS. The Shaping of Jewish History. A Radical New Interpretation. New York, 1971.

USQUE, SAMUEL. A Consolation for the Tribulations of Israel. Third Dialogue (Translator, Gershon I. Gelbart) New York, 1964.

USQUE, SAMUEL. Consolation for the Tribulations of Israel (Translator, Martin A. Cohen) Philadelphia, 1965.

HISTORY, *Ancient*

AUERBACH, ELIAS. Wüste und Gelobtes Land. Geschichte Israels von den Anfängen bis zum Tode Salomos. Berlin, 1932.

ERBT, WILHELM. Das Judentum. Die Wahrheit über seine Entstehung. Detmold, 1921.

[*Shapira Scroll*] HARRY, MYRIAM [pseudonym of SIONA SHAPIRA] A Springtide in Palestine. Boston and New York, 1924.

HISTORY, *Medieval*

DUKES, LEOPOLD. Philosophisches aus dem zehnten Jahrhundert. Ein Beitrag zur Literaturgeschichte der Mohamedaner und Juden. Nakel, 1868.

HISTORY, *Modern*

CHAZAN, ROBERT AND RAPHAEL, MARC LEE (editors) Modern Jewish History. A Source Reader. New York, 1974.

GRAYZEL, SOLOMON. A History of the Contemporary Jews from 1900 to the present. New York and Philadelphia, 1960.

JOSEPHUS FLAVIUS

(JOSEPHUS FLAVIUS) Giosefo. Il quale, con memorabil' esempio della divina giustitia, contiene l'assedio, et ultima destruttione di Gierusalem... Vinegia, 1552.

HEGESIPPUS. De bello judaico, et urbis Hierosolymitanae excidio, libri quinq;... Coloniae, 1559.

JUDAICA AMERICANA I, *to 1850*

Compendium of the Order of the Burial Service, and Rules for the Mourners, &c.... New York (1827) *Rosenbach, 291.*

CRAWFORD, CHARLES. An Essay on the Propagation of the Gospel; in which there are numerous facts and arguments Adduced to prove that many of the Indians in America Are descended from the Ten Tribes. Philadelphia, 1801. *Rosenbach, 123.*

[*La Créquinière, de*] The Agreement of the Customs of the East-Indians, with those of the Jews, and other Ancient People... London, 1705. *Roth, B17/6.*

CUMBERLAND, RICHARD. The Jew: or, Benevolent Hebrew. A Comedy, as performed with universal applause, at the New Theatre, in Philadelphia. Philadelphia, 1795. *Rosenbach, 101.*

[*Faria*] The information of Francisco de Faria, Delivered at the Bar of the House of Commons, Munday the First day of November... 1680... London, 1680. *Roth, B3/1. "Francisco de Faria, Born in America, Son of John de Faria a Jew..."*

FLEURY, CLAUDE. Manners of the Ancient Israelites:... New York, 1832. *Not in Rosenbach.*

FREY, JOSEPH SAMUEL C. F. A New Edition of a Hebrew Grammar, Considerably Altered, and Much Enlarged. New York, 1823. *Rosenbach, 238.*

Hebrew Customs; or the Missionary's Return. Philadelphia [1834] *Rosenbach, 374.*

[HOLFORD, GEORGE PETER] The Destruction of Jerusalem an absolute and irresistible Proof of the Divine Origin of Christianity... Burlington, New Jersey, 1807. *Rosenbach, 140.*

(JAHN, JOHANN) Jahn's History of the Hebrew Commonwealth; Translated from the German by Calvin E. Stowe. Andover and New York, 1828. *Rosenbach, 298.*

LINDO, A. A. A Retrospect of the Past... Cincinnati, 1848. *Rosenbach, 637.*

MACGOWAN, JOHN. The Life of Joseph, the Son of Israel. In Eight Books... Greenfield, Massachusetts, 1805.

[MARKS, DAVID] The Life of David Marks, To the 26th year of his age. Including the particulars of his conversion, call to the ministry... Written by himself. Limerick, Maine, 1831. *This edition not in Rosenbach.*

PALFREY, JOHN GORHAM. Academical Lectures on the Jewish Scriptures and Antiquities. Volumes I and II. Boston, 1838–1840. *Rosenbach, 433. Volumes III and IV were published in 1852.*

PHELPS, SAMUEL M. The Triumphs of Divine Grace, a Poem... A Description of the Millennial Reign of Jesus Christ on Earth, by a Converted Israelite. New York, 1835.

SMITH, ELIAS. The Whole World Governed by a Jew; or the Government of the Second Adam, as King and Priest... Exeter, 1805. *Wolf, 25.*

TAPPAN, DAVID. Lectures on Jewish Antiquities; Delivered at Harvard University in Cambridge... Boston, 1807. *Rosenbach, 144.*

WOOD, THOMAS. The Mosaic History of the Creation of the World... New York, 1831. *Rosenbach, 340.*

JUDAICA AMERICANA II, *from 1851*

BIRMINGHAM, STEPHEN. The Grandees. America's Sephardic Elite. New York, etc., 1971.

[*Cohn, Harry*] THOMAS, BOB. King Cohn. The Life and Times of Harry Cohn. London, 1967.

[*Cohen, Morris R.*] DEREGIBUS, ARTURO. Il razionalismo di Morris R. Cohen nella filosofia americana d'oggi. Torino, 1960.

GLANZ, RUDOLF. Jews in Relation to the Cultural Milieu of the Germans in America up to the Eighteen Eighties. New York, 1947.

GLANZ, RUDOLF. Studies in Judaica Americana. New York, 1970.

GOLDFARB, SAM. How from a Monkey I became a Man. Sarasota, Florida, 1964.

GOMPERS, SAM[UEL] Letter Signed, 1 page. Washington, District of Columbia, March 31, 1899. To Hamilton Holt [editor, *The Independent*] New York.

HARPER, WILLIAM R. American Institute of Hebrew. The Hebrew Correspondence School. Progressive Course. Lesson 1–40. Morgan Park, Chicago, no date.

JICK, LEON A. (editor) The Teaching of Judaica in American Universities. The Proceedings of a Colloquium (New York) 1970.

KAHN, OTTO H. Le droit au-dessus de la race. Paris, 1919.

KARFF, SAMUEL E. (editor) Hebrew Union College-Jewish Institute of Religion At One Hundred Years (Cincinnati, Ohio) 1976.

KORN, BERTRAM WALLACE. German-Jewish Intellectual Influences on American Jewish Life, 1824–1972. Syracuse, 1972.

LEBESON, ANITA LIBMAN. Recall to Life. The Jewish Woman in America. New York and London, 1970.

LONDON, HANNAH R. Shades of My Forefathers. Springfield, Massachusetts, 1941. *Limited signed edition.*

LUMER, HYMAN. The "Jewish Defense League" A New Face for Reaction. New York, 1971.

MARCUS, JACOB R. (editor) Critical Studies in American Jewish History. 3 volumes. Cincinnati, Ohio and New York, 1971.

[*Morgenthau, Henry*] LEBOW, RICHARD NED. The Morgenthau Peace Mission of 1917 [New York] 1970. *Offprint.*

ROSENBACH, A. S. W. A Book Hunter's Holiday. Adventures with Books and Manuscripts. Cambridge, 1936. *Autographed.*

[*Rosenberg*] SCHEER, MAXIMILIAN. Ethel und Julius. Berlin, 1954.

[*Rosenfeld*] D'ESAGUY, AUGUSTO. The Tragic Life and Poetry of Morris Rosenfeld. Lisboa, 1950.

[*Schiff*] ARNSBERG, PAUL. Jakob H. Schiff. Von der Frankfurter Judengasse zur Wallstreet. Frankfurt am Main, 1969.

JEWISH QUESTION IN USA

[*Coughlin*] MAGIL, A. B. The Real Father Coughlin. New York, 1939.

GILBERT, ARTHUR. A Jew in Christian America. New York, 1966.

LEVINGER, LEE J. Anti-Semitism in the United States. Its History and Causes. New York, 1925.

MCWILLIAMS, CAREY. A Mask for Privilege: Anti-Semitism in America. Boston, 1948.

HENRY FORD

FORD, HENRY. Der internationale Jude. 2 volumes. Leipzig, no date.

ANGLO-JUDAICA I, *to 1850*

[*Hirschel, Solomon*] Order of Service for the Funeral of the Lamented Chief Rabbi, Rev. Solomon Hirschel . . . 5603. London [1843]

Jewish Superstition inconsistent with Christian Liberty. Being a Dissertation on the Apostolick Council at Jerusalem . . . London, 1736.

MELDOLA, D. Form of Prayer and Thanksgiving . . . for the Merciful Preservation of Her Most Gracious Majesty and Her Illustrious Consort. London [1840]

MORNAY, PHILIPPE DE. A Worke Concerning the trunesse of the Christian Religion: Against . . . Jews . . . London, 1617. *Fourth edition. Roth, B6/2.*

PRIESTLEY, JOSEPH. Letters to the Jews; Inviting them to an Amicable Discussion of the Evidences of Christianity. Birmingham, 1787. *Second edition, with Part II added. Roth, B4/23.*

ROBERTSON, WILLIAM . . . A Gate or Door to the Holy Tongue, Opened in English. London, 1653. *Roth, B15/17.*

ANGLO-JUDAICA II, *from 1851*

BENTWICH, NORMAN. Anglo-Jewish Causes Célèbres . . . [London, 1946] *Photostatic offprint.*

FISCH, HAROLD. Jerusalem and Albion. The Hebraic Factor in Seventeenth-Century Literature. London, 1964.

FRIEDMAN, LEE M. "A Jewes Prophesy" and Caleb Shilock. Boston, 1947. *Offprint.*

[*Laski, Harold*] MARTIN, KINGSLEY. Harold Laski (1893–1950) a biographical memoir. London, 1953.

LEVIN, SALMOND S. (editor) A Century of Anglo-Jewish Life 1870–1970. London [1973]

Memorial Service . . . 1936 the Day of the Funeral of His Late Majesty King George (Great Synagogue, Duke Street, London) London (1936)

Migration and Settlement. Proceedings of the Anglo-American Jewish Historical Conference . . . 1970. London, 1971.

Order of Service of Thanksgiving and Dedication to commemorate The Tercentenary of the Resettlement of Jewry in the British Isles in 1656 . . . Manchester . . . 1956. Manchester (1956)

Prayer of Thanksgiving on the occasion of the Three Hundredth Anniversary of the Resettlement of Jews in England . . . 1956 (Tercentenary Sabbath) London (1956)

Prayer & Thanksgiving for the Coronation of Her Majesty Queen Elizabeth II . . . 1953. Order of Service. Birmingham, 1953.

Prayer and Thanksgiving for the Coronation of Her Majesty Queen Elizabeth . . . 1953. Manchester, 1953.

[*Reading*] WALKER-SMITH, DEREK. Lord Reading and his Cases: the Study of a Great Career. New York, 1934.

ROTH, CECIL. The Rise of Provincial Jewry. The Early History of the Jewish Communities in the English Countryside, 1740–1840. London, 1950.

SILBERMAN, HILDA. Unimportant Letters of Important Years 1941–1951. London (1951)

Tercentenary Banquet in Guildhall to celebrate the Three-hundredth Anniversary of the Re-settlement of the Jews in the British Isles (London) 1956.

EMANCIPATION IN ENGLAND

BIRKS, T. R. A Letter to . . . Lord John Russell, M.P. on the Admission of Jews to Parliament. London, 1848. *Roth, B1/224.*

A Collection of Testimonies in Favor of Religious Liberty, in the Case of the Dissenters, Catholics, and Jews. By a Christian Politician. London, 1790. *Roth, B1/138.*

EDISON, JOHN SIBBALD. The Question of the Admissibility of the Jews to Parliament as yet Undecided. London, 1859. *Roth, B1/268a.*

GRANT, ROBERT [etc.] Speeches . . . in the House of Commons, . . . Relative to the Civil Disabilities of the Jews. London, 1833. *Roth, B1/181.*

PERCEVAL, DUDLEY M. Maynooth and the Jew Bill . . . London and Edinburgh, 1845. *Roth, B1/206.*

[*Toland*] BARZILAY, ISAAC E. John Toland's Borrowings from Simone Luzzatto. New York, 1969. *Offprint.*

MOSES MONTEFIORE

FIEBERMANN, JOSEF. Sir Moses Montefiore Bart. Frankfurt am Main, 1884. *Offprint.*

LEVIN, M. Moses Montefiore. Rede zu dessen hundertjähriger Geburtsfeier . . . 1884. Berlin, 1885.

SCHIFFER, S. Sir Moses Chaim Montefiore. Halberstadt, 1878.

Traduzione del Firmano accordato da Sua Maesta' Imperiale Il Sultano Abd-ool-Medjid agli Israeliti del suo impero a richiesta del cavaliere Sir Moses Montefiore . . . Malta, 1840.

WESTON, JAMES. Sir Moses Montefiore; The Story of his Life. London, no date.

MENASSEH BEN ISRAEL

MENASSEH BEN ISRAEL. Mikveh Israel Hoc est, Spes Israelis. Amstelodami, 1650. *First edition. Da Silva Rosa, 57a; Roth, B1/8; Life, page 186.*

MANASSEH BEN ISRAEL. Rettung der Juden. Aus dem Englischen übersetzt. Nebst einer Vorrede von Moses Mendelssohn. Berlin and Stettin, 1782. *Da Silva Rosa, 66.*

MANASSEH BEN ISRAEL. De Verlossing der Jooden . . . met een Voorreden verrykt door Moses Mendelssohn . . . s'Gravenhage, 1782. *Second Dutch edition of Vindiciae Judaeorum.*

LORD GEORGE GORDON

A Narrative of the Proceedings of Lord Geo. Gordon, and the Persons Assembled under the Denomination of the Protestant Association, from their Last Meeting at Coach-Makers Hall, to the final Commitment of his Lordship to the Tower . . . London, 1780. *Roth, B3/31.*

The Trial of the Right Honourable George Gordon, Commonly called Lord George Gordon, on a Bill of Indictment for High Treason; in the Court of King's Bench, Westminster . . . Taken in Short-Hand . . . By a Member of the Middle Temple. London, no date [1781?] *This edition not in Roth.*

ISAAC DISRAELI

D'ISRAELI [ISAAC] Autograph Letter, 1 page, written in the third person, dated June 5, no year to Mr. Du Bois.

D'ISRAELI, I. Miscellanies; or, Literary Recreations. London, 1796. *First edition. Roth, B20/62.*

D'ISRAELI, I. Narrative Poems. London, 1803. *First edition.*

D'ISRAELI, I. A Second Series of Curiosities of Literature . . . 3 volumes. London, 1823. *Roth, B20/56.*

CORNEY, BOLTON. Curiosities of Literature by I. D' Israeli, Esq. . . . Illustrated. London, 1838.

OGDEN, JAMES. Isaac D'Israeli. Oxford, 1969.

DISRAELI, ISAAC. The Invention of Printing. The American Institute of Graphic Arts, 1940.

DISRAELI, ISAAC. The Invention of Printing. Cincinnati, Ohio, 1942.

DISRAELI, ISAAC. The First English Printer. Cincinnati, Ohio, 1942.

DISRAELI, ISAAC. The War Against Books. Cincinnati, Ohio, 1942.

BENJAMIN DISRAELI

LORD BEACONSFIELD (DISRAELI) Contarini Fleming. Ein psychologischer Roman. Berlin, 1909.

Letter in unknown hand on Lord Beaconsfield's own mourning stationery concerning his funeral. "Her Majesty desires wishes in Lord Beaconsfield's will to be strictly observed."

BLAKE, ROBERT. Disraeli. New York, 1967.

CRAEMER, RUDOLF. Benjamin Disraeli. Praha, 1943.

JERMAN, B. R. The Young Disraeli. Princeton, New Jersey, 1960.

SOMERVELL, D. C. Disraeli & Gladstone. London, 1925.

ISRAEL ZANGWILL

ZANGWILL, ISRAEL. Ghetto Comedies. New York and London, 1907. *Presentation copy.*

ZANGWILL, ISRAEL. Ghetto-Historier. København, 1908.

ZANGWILL, ISRAEL. Nye Ghetto-Fortaellinger. København, 1908.

ZANGWILL, ISRAEL. Had Gadya. Paris, 1921.

ZANGWILL, ISRAEL. Italian Fantasies. New York, 1910.

ZANGWILL, ISRAEL. Jinny the Carrier. London, 1919.

ZANGWILL, ISRAEL. The Problem of the Jewish Race. New York, no date.

ZANGWILL, ISRAELE. Teatro. La lizza dei galli – La serra calda – Il crogiuolo. Milano (1924)

ZANGWILL, ISRAEL. Träumer des Ghetto. Berlin, 1922.

ZANGWILL, ISRAEL. La voix de Jérusalem. Paris, 1926.

ZANGWILL, I. The Grey Wig. Stories and Novelettes. New York, 1923.

(ZANGWILL, ISRAEL) Pictures of Jewish Life. From Israel Zangwill, Children of the Ghetto (editor, Philipp Aronstein) Berlin, 1935.

BRITISH-ISRAEL

THOMPSON, P. W. Israel in Prophecy and History. London, 1927.

FRANCE I, *to 1850*

PEZRON, PAUL. Défense de l'antiquité des tems, . . . où l'on fait voir la corruption de l'Hébreu des Juifs. Paris, 1691.

THIERY [ADOLPHE] Dissertation sur cette question: Est-il des moyens de rendre les Juifs plus heureux et plus utiles en France? Ouvrage couronné par la Société Royale des Sciences et des Arts de Metz. Paris, 1788.

FRANCE II, *from 1851*

[*Alliance*] Bericht über die Tätigkeit der Alliance Israélite Universelle im Jahre 1907 [Berlin, 1908]

[*Benda*] SAROCCHI, JEAN. Julien Benda. Portrait d'un Intellectuel. Paris, 1968.

BLUMENKRANZ, BERNHARD (editor) Histoire des Juifs en France. Toulouse, 1972.

GRUNEBAUM BALLIN, PAUL. La séparation des églises et de l'état. Paris, 1905.

PRADO-GAILLARD, HENRI. La condition des Juifs dans l'ancienne France. Paris, 1942.

RENAN, ERNEST. La Chaire d'Hébreu au Collège de France. Explications a mes collègues. Paris, 1862.

ROBLIN, MICHEL. Les Juifs de Paris. Démographie – Economie – Culture. Paris, 1952.

[*Stavisky*] PALUMBO, FRANCESCO. Stavisky. Milano, 1934–XII.

SZAJKOWSKI, ZOSA. Analytical Franco-Jewish Gazetteer 1939–1945. New York, 1966.

WEILL, ALEXANDRE. Nos Fiançailles. Confessions de Jeunesse . . . Paris, 1883.

EMANCIPATION IN FRANCE

Adresse des Juifs Alsaciens au Peuple d'Alsace. No place, no date [1790] *Szajkowski, Em. 120.*

[*Grégoire*] NECHELES, RUTH F. The Abbé Grégoire and the Jews (New York) 1971. *Offprint.*

GRUNEBAUM-BALLIN, P. L'Abbé Grégoire et les Juifs (Paris) 1931.

Mémoire pour les Juifs de Luneville et de Sarguemines. A Nosseigneurs de l'Assemblée Nationale. No place [1789] *Szajkowski, Em. 11.*

Recueil de pièces relatives à l'admission des Juifs à l'état civil. Paris, 1790. *Szajkowski, Em. 147.*

VOLTAIRE

FINDLAY, ROBERT. A Vindication of the Sacred Books and of Josephus . . . from Various Misrepresentations and Cavils of the Celebrated M.de Voltaire. Glasgow, 1770.

GUÉNÉE [ANTOINE] Lettres de quelques Juifs Portugais, Allemands et Polonais, à M. de Voltaire . . . Versailles, 1817.

[GUÉNÉE, ANTOINE] Lettres de quelques Juifs Portugais, Allemands et Polonais, à M. de Voltaire . . . 3 volumes. Lyon, 1822.

GUÉNÉE [ANTOINE] Lettres de quelques Juifs Allemands et Polonais à M. de Voltaire . . . 5 volumes. Paris, 1826.

FRANCE:
NAPOLEONICA AND SANHEDRIN

COHEN, BENJAMIN (composer) Ode presentée a sa Majesté Louis Napoléon, Roi de Hollande, a son arrivée a Amsterdam, ville capitale du Royaume, pour fixer sa residence. Amsterdam, 1808. *Not in Szajkowski.*

COLOGNA, ABRAHAM DE. Discours prononcé . . . Le 23 Mai 1813, A l'occasion des actions de grâces rendues à l'Eternel, pour la grande victoire remportée par l'armée Française au camp de Lutzen. Paris, 1813. *Szajkowski, Nap. 198.*

KOBLER, FRANZ. Napoleon and the Jews. New York, 1976.

[*Königreich Westphalen*] Bekanntmachung wegen besserer Einrichtung des Gottesdienstes in den Synagogen des Königreichs Westphalen. Kassel, 1810.

[*Königreich Westphalen*] MERKEL, S. F. Rede bei der Eröffnung des Königlich – Westphälischen Konsistoriums der Israeliten . . . Kassel, 1808.

JEWISH QUESTION IN FRANCE

["BLUEMCHEN, ISAAC"] Das Recht der Höheren Rasse (Le droit de la race supérieure) Eine Übersetzung aus dem Französischen von Eugen Holweg. Stuttgart (1923)

DAUDET, LÉON. Le Pays des Parlementeurs. Paris, no date [1901] *Dedicated to Edouard Drumont.*

GROOS, RENÉ (editor) Enquête sur le problème juif. Paris, no date.

[*Morès*] DRESDEN, DONALD. The Marquis de Morès: Emperor of the Bad Lands. Norman, Oklahoma, 1970.

[*Morès*] DROULERS, CHARLES. Le Marquis de Morès 1858–1896. Paris, 1932.

[*Morès*] PASCAL, FÉLICIEN. L'Assassinat de Morès. Un crime d'état. Paris, 1902.

[*Morès*] TWETON, D. JEROME. The Marquis de Morès. Dakota Capitalist. French Nationalist. Fargo, 1972.

DREYFUS AFFAIR

BARLOW, GEORGE. A History of the Dreyfus Case. From the Arrest of Captain Dreyfus in October, 1894, up to the Flight of Esterhazy in September, 1898. London, 1899. *Desachy, 55.*

CHAPMAN, GUY. The Dreyfus Trials. London, 1972.

DAUDET, LÉON. L'avant-guerre. Études et documents sur l'espionnage juif-allemand en France depuis l'Affaire Dreyfus. Paris, 1913.

FORTUNIO [pseudonym of PAULIN NIBOYET] Il dramma Alfredo Dreyfus. Milano, 1899. *Desachy, 290; Lipschutz, 501.*

GOHIER, URBAIN. L'Armée contre la Nation. Paris, 1899. *Desachy, 309.*

GUYOT, YVES. Analyse de l'enquête. Paris, 1899. *Desachy, 334.*

[LEBLOIS, HENRI-LOUIS] L'Instruction Fabre et les décisions judiciaires ultérieures. Paris [1901?] *Desachy, 375.*

[*Leblois*] DESACHY, PAUL. Une grande figure de l'Affaire Dreyfus. Louis Leblois. Paris, 1934. *Lipschutz, 154.*

LISPSCHUTZ, LÉON [*recte:* LIPSCHUTZ] Une bibliothèque dreyfusienne. Essai de Bibliographie thématique et analytique de l'affaire Dreyfus. Paris, 1970.

MARRUS, MICHAEL R. The Politics of Assimilation. A Study of the French Jewish Community at the Time of the Dreyfus Affair. Oxford, 1971.

MATULL, CURT. Sensationell ! Wird Dreyfus verurtheilt? Berlin, no date.

SALMON, ANDRÉ. L'Affaire Dreyfus. Paris, 1934. *Lipschutz, 345.*

SNYDER, LOUIS L. The Dreyfus Case. New Brunswick, New Jersey, 1973.

THOMAS, MARCEL. L'Affaire sans Dreyfus. Paris, 1961. *Lispschutz, 246.*

HENRI BERGSON

BERGSON, HENRI. Einführung in die Metaphysik. Jena, 1920.

BERGSON, HENRI. Zeit und Freiheit. Eine Abhandlung über die unmittelbaren Bewusstseinstatsachen. Jena, 1920.

ADOLPHE, LYDIE. L'Univers bergsonien. Paris, 1955.

AROUET, FRANÇOIS. La fin d'une parade philosophique: Le bergsonisme. Paris, 1929.

DESAYMARD, JOSEPH. La pensée d'Henri Bergson. Paris (1913)

LEHRMANN, CHANAN. Bergsonisme et Judaïsme. Genève, 1937.

MARIETTI, ANGÈLE. Les formes du mouvement chez Bergson. No place (1953)

MILHAUD, JEAN. A Bergson. La patrie reconnaissante [Paris] 1967.

MOSSÉ-BASTIDE, ROSE-MARIE. Bergson et Plotin. Paris, 1959.

PALGEN, RUDOLF. Die Weltanschauung Henri Bergsons. Breslau, 1929.

ROBINET, ANDRÉ. Bergson. Paris, 1965.

ZARAGÜETA, JUAN. La intuición en la filosofia de Henri Bergson. Madrid, 1941.

SWITZERLAND

[*Jacob*] CAWIL, H. Der Fall Jacob. Zürich, 1935.

Jüdisches Jahrbuch für die Schweiz. 1916/17, Luzern (1916); 1921/22, Basel (1921)

KAHN, LUDWIG DAVID. Die Nachkommen des Simon Guggenheim (1730–1799) von Endingen (Basel) 1969.

ITALY

AMINTA, FILIPPO. L'ebraisimo [*sic*] senza replica... Roma, 1823.

ANTONJ, VINCENZO BERNI DEGLI. Osservazioni... nella causa di simultanea successione di Cristiani, e di Ebrei alla intestata Eredità di un loro congiunto [Bologna] 1827. *Freimann, page 362.*

ANTONJ, VINCENZO BERNI DEGLI. Risposta... nella quistione di simultanea consuccessione di Cristiani, e di Ebrei alla intestata Eredità di un loro congiunto Cristiano. Bologna, 1827. *Freimann, page 363.*

BEDARIDA, GUIDO. Ebrei di Livorno. Tradizioni e Gergo in 180 Sonetti Giudaico-Livornesi. Firenze, 1956.

CANTONI, LELIO. Salmo di Laudi per la solenne inaugurazione del busto di S. M. il clementissimo Francesco I. d'Austria eretto... Mantova... 1828. Verona, 1828.

CESSI, ROBERTO. La condizione degli ebrei banchieri in Padova nei secoli XIV e XV. Padova, 1908. *Offprint.*

CIANTES, GIOSEFFO. Della incarnazione del verbo divino Euidentemente difesa dalle opposizioni degli Ebrei... Roma, 1668.

Curiosa istoria della bella Esther, racconto storico accaduto nell' anno 1663... nella città di Fincs (Polonia)... Gerusalemme, 1894.

GATTI, GIUSEPPE. La rigenerazione politica degli Israeliti in Italia. Casale, 1848.

LEVI, BELLOM. Ode in Lingua Ebraica in Occasione dell' Augusta Comparsa delle LL.SS. E RR.MM. Napoleone Primo e Giuseppina nella Citta' di Casale... Casale, no date.

[*Livorno*] Preghiere recitate, e cantate nel Tempio degli Ebrei di Livorno... 1808. Ricorrendo il faustissimo Giorno Natalizio di S.M.I., e R. l'augustissimo Napoleone I. Imperatore de' Francesi, Re d'Italia, e Protettore della Confederazione del Reno... [with an ode by Salomone Fiorentino] Livorno, 1808. *Szajkowski, 212.*

LUCHINI, ODOARDO. Perchè la legislazione ebraica non poté ammettere la facoltà di testare. Introduzione storica alla interpetrazione di alcuni testi talmudici. Firenze, 1880.

LUZZATTI, LUIGI. Grandi italiani grandi sacrifici per la patria (Opere di Luigi Luzzatti, volume primo) Bologna (1924)

LUZZATTI, LUIGI. La paix monétaire à la conférence de Gênes. Roma, 1922.

[*Luzzatti, Luigi*] Catalogo della Biblioteca "Luigi Luzzatti" (Roma) 1924.

BEHAR, YAKIR. Luigi Luzzatti. Prato, 1928.

[*Luzzatto, Samuel David*] La rassegna mensile di Israel. Nel primo centenario della scomparsa di Samuel David Luzzatto. Milano and Roma, 1966.

[*Luzzatto, Simone*] BARZILAY, ISAAC E. John Toland's Borrowings from Simone Luzzatto. New York, 1969. *Offprint.*

PANZINI, ALFREDO. Viaggio con la giovane ebrea. Milano, 1935–XIII.

PICHI, PIETRO. Le stolte dottrine de gli Ebrei con la loro confutatione. Roma, 1640.

PINETTI, ANGELO. Una supplica alla Serenissima [Republica di Venezia] contro gli ebrei. Venezia (1900) *Reprint.*

Nuove Regole imposte dall'Università degli Ebrei di Modena per norma de'loro singoli... Modena, 1796.

ROMANO, MANOELLO. I teologi naturali. Squarcio del Paradiso. Versione dall'ebraico (Per le nozze del Professore Alessandro d'Ancona con la gentilissima damigella Adele Nissim) Pisa, 1871.

ROTH, CECIL. Gli Ebrei a Firenze sotto l'ultima repubblica. Firenze, 1924.

ROTH, CECIL. Léon de Modène, ses Riti Ebraici et le Saint Office a Venise. Paris, 1929.

SARAVAL, JACOB RAFFAEL. Viaggi in Olanda. Venezia, 1807. *Fürst III, page 244.*

SCHAERF, SAMUELE. I Cognomi degli Ebrei d'Italia... Firenze, 1925.

Sposalizio della gnora Luna col sor Baruccabà e mortc di essa per il gran disturbo avuto nel suo Sposalizio. Lucca, no date.

Seconde nozze di Baruccabà con la bella Diana infedele, e fuga di essa con due Mercanti, e morte dello sposo Baruccabà e del rabbino, ed il suo ritrovamento in Venezia, abbandonata dalli due Mercanti. Lucca, no date.

SHULVASS, MOSES A. The Jews in the World of the Renaissance. Leiden and Chicago, 1973.

SONNINO, SIDNEY. Finanza e politica. Discorsi . . . Roma, 1891.

SONNINO, SIDNEY. Del governo rappresentativo in Italia. Roma, 1872.

SONNINO, SIDNEY. La politica finanziaria. Discorso . . . Roma, 1891.

SONNINO, SIDNEY. Il suffragio universale in Italia. Firenze, 1870.

VICCEI, ANGELO ANTONIO. Il pasto degli Ebrei. Opera vaga, e dilettevole, divisa in quattro parti. Loreto, 1779.

ROME

Dissertazione sopra il commercio, usure, e condotta degli Ebrei nello Stato Pontifico. Roma, 1826. *Freimann, page 302.*

CARPI, LEON. Blocco dei francesi al ghetto di Roma nell'anno di grazia 1849 e secondo della loro Repubblica. Torino, 1849.

GELLER, HENRYK (and ARD and RUTH LILIANA) Roma Ebraica. Duemila anni in immagini. Jewish Rome. A pictorial history of 2000 years. Rome, 1970.

JEWISH QUESTION IN ITALY

ASCOLI, ROBERTO. L'antisemitismo in Italia. Cause e rimedi. Modena, 1904.

ORREI, ERNESTO. Intorno alla questione ebraica. Lineamenti di storia e di dottrina. Roma [1942] *Date misprinted.*

PREZIOSI, GIOVANNI. Come il giudaismo ha preparato la guerra. Roma, 1939–XVIII.

RIGHINI, EUGENIO. Antisemitismo e semitismo nell' Italia politica moderna. Palmermo and Milano, 1901.

CESARE LOMBROSO

LOMBROSO, CESARE. Psicologia e natura. Torino, 1927.

LOMBROSO, CESARE. L'Uomo bianco e l'uomo di colore. Padova, 1871.

AUSTRIA I, *to 1850*

Die Landtagsverhandlungen über die bürgerliche Stellung der Juden in Preussen. Mit Beziehung auf Oesterreich. Leipzig, 1847. *Eichstädt, 1933.*

REALIS (pseudonym of GERHARD ROBERT WALTER VON CÖCKELBERGHE-DÜTZELE) Die Juden und die Judenstadt in Wien. Wien, 1846.

ROHRER, JOSEPH. Versuch über die jüdischen Bewohner der österreichischen Monarchie. Wien, 1804.

[SCHIRNDING, FERDINAND] Das Judenthum in Oesterreich und die böhmischen Unruhen. Leipzig, 1845. *Eichstädt, 1977.*

AUSTRIA II, *from 1851*

[*Altenberg*] KRAUS, KARL. Peter Altenberg (Rede am Grabe Peter Altenbergs 11. Januar 1919) Wien (1919)

BENEDIKT, MORITZ. Aus meinem Leben. Erinnerungen und Erörterungen. Wien, 1906.

[*Bloch, Joseph*] GRUNWALD, MAX (editor) Dr. Josef S. Bloch. Auswahl aus seiner Briefsammlung. Wien, 1930.

ELBOGEN, HEINRICH. Friedensgedanken eines Heimkehrers. Schloss Thalheim, 1928.

[*Gomperz*] WEINBERG, ADELAIDE. Theodor Gomperz and John Stuart Mill. Genève, 1963.

HERZOG, D. (editor) Quellen und Forschungen zur Geschichte der Juden in der Steiermark. 1. Band: Urkunden und Regesten zur Geschichte der Juden in der Steiermark (1475–1585) Graz, 1934. *All published?*

[*Königswarter*] KOPFSTEIN, SIGMUND. Ein Glaubenszwist im Hause Königswarter. Wien, 1895.

LANDAU, SAUL RAPHAEL. Fort mit den Hausjuden! Grundlinien jüdischer Volkspolitik. Wien, 1907.

ROSENBERG, ARTUR. Beiträge zur Geschichte der Juden in Steiermark. Wien and Leipzig, 1914.

SCHNITZLER, ARTHUR. Gesammelte Werke. Erste Abteilung: Die erzählenden Schriften, 3 volumes. Zweite Abteilung: Die Theaterstücke, 4 volumes. 7 volumes. Berlin, 1912.

[*Sonnenfels*] MÜLLER, WILIBALD. Josef von Sonnenfels. Biographische Studie aus dem Zeitalter der Aufklärung in Oesterreich. Wien, 1882.

WACHSTEIN, BERNHARD. Gottlieb Saphirs Testament. Wien, 1918. *Offprint.*

WEISL, WOLFGANG VON. Die Juden in der Armee Österreich-Ungarns. Illegale Transporte. Skizze zu einer Autobiographie. Tel Aviv, 1971.

BOHEMIA, MORAVIA AND CZECHOSLOVAKIA

Czechoslovakia and the Czechoslovak Jews. Addresses Delivered at the Meeting of the Czechoslovak Jewish Representative Committee . . . (1944) New York, 1945.

(HEŘMAN, JAN) Der alte jüdische Friedhof in Prag. Prag, no date.

JACOBI, WALTER. Golem . . . Geissel der Tschechen. Die Zersetzung des tschechischen Nationalismus. Prag, 1942.

[*Jellinek, Oskar*] KREJČI, KAREL. Oskar Jellinek Leben und Werk (22.1.1886–12.10.1949) Brno, 1967.

The Jews of Czechoslovakia. Historical Studies and Surveys. 2 volumes. Philadelphia and New York, 1968–1971.

[*Kafka*] Franz Kafka 1883–1924. An Exhibition . . . Berlin (1968) *Catalogue.*

[*Masaryk*] LÖWY, RUDOLF. Trauerrede gehalten anlässlich des Hinscheidens des Befreier-Präsidenten T. G. Masaryk im Tempel zu Bardejov . . . Bardejov, 1937. *German and Slovak.*

[TELLER, M.] Die Juden in Böhmen und ihre Stellung in der Gegenwart. Prag, 1863. *Muneles, 903.*

HUNGARY

BÖHM, CARL. Empfindungen der Israeliten bey der festlichen Installation des . . . Herrn Johann Nep. Aloys Freyherrn Malonyay von Vicsap . . . in die Obergespanns-Würde des löbl. Neutraer Komitats . . . 1825 . . . Tyrnau (1825)

KEMMEL, LÖWLE (pseudonym?) Helden-Lied über die Königin in Ungarn und Jhre Gnade gegen die Juden. No place, 1745.

REICH, IGNAZ (editor) Beth-Lechem. Jahrbuch zur Beförderung des Ackerbaues, Handwerks und der Industrie unter den Israeliten Ungarns. 2 volumes. Volume 1: Pest, 1871; Volume 2: Budapest, 1873.

HOLLAND

COHEN, BENJAMIN (composer) Ode presentée à sa Majesté Louis Napoléon, Roi de Hollande, à son arrivée à Amsterdam, ville capitale du Royaume, pour fixer sa residence. Amsterdam, 1808.

[*Hiegentlich*] YPES, CATHARINA (editor) Een Joods artist tussen twee oorlogen. Jacob Hiegentlich 1907–1940. Amsterdam [1949]

Hymne, louanges et prières, prononcés par le Révérend Grand-Rabbin des Israélites Portugais à Amsterdam; A l'occasion de ce que Leurs Majestés Impériales et Royales l'Empereur et Roi, Napoléon le Grand, et l'Impératrice Reine, Marie Louise, daignèrent honorer de leur Auguste présence le Temple de la susdite Communauté, au mois d'Octobre 1811. Amsterdam, 1811.

PIMENTEL, HENRIQUEZ. Geschiedkundige aanteekeningen betreffende de Portugesche Israelieten in den Haag en hunne Synagogen aldaar. Gedenk-schrift . . . 'sGravenhage, 1876.

PRESSER, J. Ondergang. De vervolging en verdelging van het Nederlandse Jodendom 1940–1945. 2 volumes. 's-Gravenhage, 1965.

ROS, A. VAN. De Jood. Een waarschuwend woord aan den Christen. Roermond, 1891.

SARAVAL, JACOB RAFFAEL. Viaggi in Olanda. Venezia, 1807. *Fürst III, page 244.*

WERTHEIM, J. L. Proza en poëzie. 2 volumes. Amsterdam, 1883–1884.

By SPINOZA

[SPINOZA, BARUCH] Tractatus Theologico-Politicus, Cui adjunctus est Philosophia S. Scripturae interpres. No place, 1674. *Bamberger ("The early editions . . ." Studies in Bibliography and Booklore, volume 5) edition T.3E.*

SPINOZA, BENEDIKT VON. Über Heilige Schrift, Judenthum, Recht der höchsten Gewalt in geistlichen Dingen, und Freyheit zu philosophiren. Aus dem Lateinischen. Gera, 1787.

[MEYER, LODEWIJK] Philosophia S. Scripturae interpres; . . . Eleutheropoli [Amsterdam] 1666. *Written by Spinoza?*

On SPINOZA

BRUNSCHVICG, LÉON. Spinoza et ses contemporains. Paris, 1971.

Zum Charakter Spinozas. Erläuterung der wichtigsten Nachrichten über sein Leben. Vom Verfasser des Spinoza Redivivus . . . Halle (Saale) 1919. *See Chronicon Spinozanum III, page 351.*

FERRIÈRE, ÉMILE. La doctrine de Spinoza . . . Paris, no date.

FREYER, KURT. Spinoza. Führer der Irrenden. Gedenkschrift . . . Berlin, 1927. *Limited numbered edition.*

HAMPSHIRE, STUART. Spinoza. Hammondsworth, 1971.

SCHMIDT-BIGGEMANN, WILHELM (editor) Baruch de Spinoza 1677–1977. His Work and its Reception. Baarn (1977)

SÉROUYA, HENRI. Spinoza. Sa vie et sa philosophie. Paris, 1933.

URIEL DA COSTA

BARJITZCHAK, YOSHUAH. Uriel da Costa. Den Haag, 1962.

ISAAC DA COSTA

DA COSTA, I. Alfonsus de eerste. Treurspel. Amsterdam, 1818.

DA COSTA, I. Antwoord aan den Heer J. G. Le Sage ten Broek. Amsterdam, 1829.

DA COSTA, I. Bezwaren tegen den geest der eeuw. Leyden, 1823. *Third edition.*

DA COSTA, ISAAC. Brieven (editor, Groen van Prinsterer) 2 volumes in 1 (1830–1855) Amsterdam, 1872–1873.

DA COSTA, ISAAC. De Chaos en het Licht; een halve-eeuw-lied. Haarlem, 1850.

DA COSTA [ISAAC] Kompleete Dichtwerken. 3 volumes. Haarlem, 1861–1863.

DA COSTA, ISAAC [AND OTHERS] Noble Families among the Sephardic Jews with some Account of the Capadose Family (including their Conversion to Christianity) by Bertram Brewster . . . London, 1936.

DA COSTA, Is. Feestliederen. Amsterdam, 1846.

DA COSTA, I. God met ons. Amsterdam, 1826.

DA COSTA. Godsdienstige en Bijbelsche Poëzie (editor, Arth. Coussens) Hoogstraten, 1909.

DA COSTA, Is. Herinneringen uit het Leven en den Omgang van Willem de Clercq . . . Amsterdam, 1850.

DA COSTA, ISAAC. Israel en de volken; een overzicht van de geschiedenis der Joden tot op onzen tijd. Haarlem, 1848.

DA COSTA, ISAAC. Israel and the Gentiles. London, 1850.

DA COSTA, I. Kerst- en Nieuwjaarsintreezangen. Amsterdam, 1829.

DA COSTA, I. Dichterlijk krijgsmuzijk. Amsterdam, 1826.

DA COSTA, Is. Aan de Leden der Tweede Klasse van het Koninklijk-Nederlandsche Instituut . . . No place, 1844.

DA COSTA, Is. Het Lied van Moses. No place, no date. *Offprint.*

[DA COSTA, ISAAC] Aan Nederland. Amsterdam, 1826.

DA COSTA, ISAAC. Aan Nederland, in de Lente van 1844. Amsterdam, 1844.

DA COSTA, ISAAC. Politieke Poëzy. Haarlem, 1854.

DA COSTA, ISAAC. Rouw en Trouw. Haarlem, 1849.

DA COSTA, I. De Sadduceën. Leyden, 1824.

DA COSTA, I. De Verbondsverklaring van 1573 aan Nederland herinnerd. Amsterdam, 1831.

DA COSTA, ISAAC. Voorlezingen over de verscheidenheid en de overeenstemming der vier Evangelien . . . 2 volumes. Leiden, 1840–1842.

DA COSTA, ISAAC. Voorlezingen over de waarheid en waardij der schriften van het Oude Testament. 2 volumes. Leiden, 1844–1848.

DA COSTA, ISAAC. Wachter! Wat is er van den nacht? Een lied bij de uitgangen van 1847. Haarlem, 1848.

DA COSTA, I. Geestelijke Wapenkreet. Rotterdam, 1825.

DA COSTA, ISAAC. Zit aan mijne rechterhand. Amsterdam, 1848.

DA COSTA, ISAAC. 1648 en 1848. Dichtstuk . . . Haarlem, 1848.

BILDERDIJK, WILLEM. De bezwaren tegen den geest der eeuw van Mr. I. da Costa, toegelicht. Leyden, 1823.

BYVANCK, W. G. C. De jeugd van Isaäc da Costa (1798–1825) 2 volumes. Zutphen, no date.

CHANTEPIE DE LA SAUSSAYE, D. Rede, gehouden ter gedachtenis aan Mr. Isaac Da Costa, in de vergadering der vrienden Israels te Leyden . . . 1860. Leyden, 1860.

KOENEN, H. J. Levensberigt van Mr. Is. Da Costa. Leiden, 1860. *Offprint.*

MEIJER, JAAP. Isaac da Costa's weg naar het Christendom. Bijdrage tot de geschiedenis der joodsche problematiek in Nederland. Amsterdam, 1946.

MEIJER, JAAP. Martelgang of Cirkelgang. Isaac da Costa als Joods Romanticus. Paramaribo, Suriname, 1954.

OOSTERHOF, OKKO NANNING. Isaäc da Costa als polemist. Kampen, 1913.

OOSTERZEE, J. J. VAN. Iets over Da Costa. Rotterdam, 1861.

[OPZOOMER, C. W.] Andwoord aan Mr. I. Da Costa, ter Wederlegging van het Stukjen "Rekenschap van Gevoelens . . ." Leiden, 1843.

[PIERSON, A.] Isaac Da Costa. Een Gedenkrede. Haarlem, 1865.

ROI, JOH. DE LE. Isaak da Costa, der holländische Christ und Dichter aus Israel. Leipzig, 1899.

(SCHRÖTER, J.J.E.F.) Gedachten over de bezwaren tegen den geest der eeuw van Mr. I. da Costa. Dordrecht, 1823.

[SCHWARTZ, C.] Ter gedachtenis aan Mr. Isaac Da Costa. Amsterdam, 1860.

V., A. Een Lied des Tijds, aan de Vaderlandsche Dichters. Met eene Opdragt aan Mr. I. Da Costa. Amsterdam, 1855.

JACOB ISRAEL DE HAAN

DE HAAN, JACOB ISRAEL. Sabbath. Amsterdam, 1917. *Offprint.*

DE HAAN, MIES. Jacob Israël de Haan, mijn broer. Amsterdam, 1954.

SPAIN AND PORTUGAL

ALVAREZ-GENDIN, SABINO. Los Judios en el mundo y en España (Discurso . . .) Oviedo, 1949.

FREIRE, JOÃO PAULO (MÁRIO) Os Judeus e os protocolos dos sábios de Sião. 4 volumes. Lisboa, 1937–1939.

[*Orobio de Castro, Isaac*] D'ESAGUY, AUGUSTO. The Dramatic Life of Oróbio de Castro. No place, 1937. *Offprint.*

ORTIZ, ANTONIO DOMINGUEZ. Los Judeoconversos en España y América. Madrid, 1971.

STEINHAUS, FEDERICO. Ebraismo Sefardita. Storia degli Ebrei di Spagna nel medio evo. Bologna, 1969.

SCANDINAVIA

BALSLEV, BENJ. De danske Jøders Historie. København, 1932.

BASTHOLM (DR.) Skrivelse i Anledning af De Herrer Repraesentantere for den jødiske Menighed i Kiøbenhavn, Deres Skrivelse til Medborgerne af den christne Troe. Kiøbenhavn, 1813.

BERTELSEN, AAGE. Oktober 43. Ereignisse und Erlebnisse während der Judenverfolgung in Dänemark. München, 1960.

BRUUN, T. C. Ikke om Jøderne, men deres Gienløser, Justitsraaden. Kiøbenhavn, 1813.

CHRISTENSEN, C. Ere Jøderne skadelige eller nyttige for Staten? Kjøbenhavn, 1813.

[*Ekelund*] KLEIN, WALTER. Var Vilhelm Ekelund antisemit? Uddevalla, 1964. *Limited numbered edition.*

ETTLINGER, J. Programm für die Trauerfeier wegen Ablebens Seiner Majestät des Königs Christian VIII. am Tage der Beisetzung . . . 1848. Altona (1848)

HARTVIG, MICHAEL. Jøderne i Danmark i tiden 1600–1800. København, 1951.

[*Nathanson*] Kurzer Abriss von L. M. Nathanson's unerhörten Schicksalen, seinem Wirken für das Wohl seines Landes u.s.w. als Erklärung zu seiner "Poetischen Klage." Altona, 1856.

SYSKIND, A., Tolv Taler holdte i den jødiske Menighed i Randers i Aarene 1834–49. Kjøbenhavn, 1896.

WOLFF, ABRAHAM ALEXANDER. Predigt am Sabbathe Emor 5589. Beim Antritte seines Amtes als Priester der mosaischen Gemeinde zu Kopenhagen . . . 1829. Darmstadt, 1829.

WOLFF, ABRAHAM ALEXANDER. Predigt . . . 1840, Auf Veranlassung des Jubelfestes der fünfundzwanzigjährigen glücklichen Verbindung . . . des Königs Christian VIII und der Königinn [*sic*] Caroline Amalia. Copenhagen (1840)

WOLFF, A. A. Zwei Predigten, auf Veranlassung des Hintritts weiland S. M. des Königs Frederiks des Sechsten . . . Copenhagen, 1840.

WOLFF, A. A. Rede bei der Einweihungsfeier der mosaischen Freischule für Knaben zu Kopenhagen, . . . 1845. Kopenhagen, 1845.

GEORGE BRANDES

BRANDES, GEORGE. Autograph Letter Signed, 1 page. Copenhagen, December 9 [18]95. To unknown addressee concerning sale of his book in America.

BERGEL, KURT (editor) Georg Brandes und Arthur Schnitzler. Ein Briefwechsel. Bern, 1956.

PROOST, K. F. Georg Brandes. Inleiding tot zijn leven en werken. Arnhem, 1940.

POLAND

Curiosa istoria della bella Esther, racconto storico accaduto nell' anno 1663 . . . nella città di Fincs (Polonia) . . . Gerusalemme, 1894.

LUMER, HYMAN. What Happened in Poland. New York, 1969.

[*Mickiewicz*] SCHEPS, SAMUEL. Adam Mickiewicz, ses affinités juives. Paris, 1964. *Presentation copy.*

SHULVASS, MOSES A. Jewish Culture in Eastern Europe. The Classical Period. New York, 1975.

VETULANI, ADAM. The Jews in Medieval Poland. No place [1962]

WEINRYB, BERNARD D. The Jews of Poland. A Social and Economic History of the Jewish Community in Poland from 1100 to 1800. Philadelphia, 1973.

WIESENTHAL, SIMON. Judenhetze in Polen (Bonn) [1968]

RUSSIA

[*Aseff*] BERNSTEIN, L. L'Affaire Azeff. Histoire et documents. Paris, 1909.

BUCHHOLTZ, ANTON. Geschichte der Juden in Riga bis zur Begründung der Rigischen Hebräergemeinde im J. 1842. Riga, 1899.

FRIEDLÄNDER, M. Fünf Wochen in Brody unter jüdischrussischen Emigranten. Ein Beitrag zur Geschichte der russischen Judenverfolgung. Wien, 1882.

LANIN, E. B. The Jews in Russia [London] 1890. *Offprint.*

NEMIROWITSCH-DANTSCHENKO. Israel in Waffen. Unter den Juden Daghestans. Leipzig, 1893.

PARETZKI, ELIE. Die Entstehung der jüdischen Arbeiterbewegung in Russland. Zandvoort, 1971. *Reprint of Riga, 1932.*

PATTERSON, DAVID. The Hebrew Novel in Czarist Russia. Edinburgh, 1964.

SCHWABACHER, SIMEON LEON v. Drei Gespenster. Eine Zeitfrage. Stuttgart, 1883.

SCHWABACHER, SIMEON LEON. Lorber, Palme, Myrthe und Cypresse. Der Kaiserpark. Festpredigten bei Allerhöchsten Veranlassungen. Odessa, 1869.

[*Schwabacher*] CH., O. Rückblick auf die Thätigkeit des Odessaer Stadtrabbiners Herrn Dr. S. L. Schwabacher bei Gelegenheit seines 25jähr. Dienstjubiläums ... 1885. Odessa, 1885.

SOVIET UNION

ABOSCH, HEINZ. Antisemitismus in Russland. Eine Analyse und Dokumentation zum sowjetischen Antisemitismus. Darmstadt, 1972.

BOLSHAKOV, V. Anti-Sovietism – Profession of Zionists. Moscow, 1971.

BOLSHAKOV, V. Anti-Communism, the Main Line of Zionism. Moscow, 1972.

FRENKEL, WLADIMIRO. Amore e bolscevismo Talmud e Khamstvo. Roma, 1922.

KOCHAN, LIONEL (editor) The Jews in Soviet Russia since 1917. London, etc., 1970.

LANDMANN, KAMILLO. Die russische Judenfrage und die Nahost-Politik der Sowjetunion. Rothenburg ob der Tauber, 1970.

NETCVOLODOW, A. Giuda senza maschera. I. Perchè l'alta banca giudaica ha finanziato la rivoluzione russa. Firenze, no date.

NILLESEN, J. A. De sociale toestand der Joden in Rusland onder de Tsaren en de Sowets. Een bijdrage tot de studie van het Jodenvraagstuk. Nijmegen-Utrecht, 1939.

RABINOVICH, SOLOMON. Jews in the Soviet Union. Moscow [1973]

SCHLOSS, ROLF W. Lass mein Volk ziehen. Die russischen Juden zwischen Sowjetstern und Davidstern. München – Wien, 1971.

Soviet Jews: Fact and Fiction. Moscow, no date. *Two textually different issues.*

Soviet Jews Reject Zionist "Protection." Novosti Press Agency Round-Table Discussion February 5, 1971. Moscow, 1971.

ROUMANIA

GOLDSMID, ANNA MARIA. Persecution of the Jews of Roumania ... London, 1872.

La question des Israélites en Roumanie. Paris, 1869.

VERAX [pseudonym] La Roumanie et les Juifs. Bucarest, 1903.

EUROPE

GALLAVARDIN. Position des Juifs dans le monde et particulièrement en France et en Allemagne ... Paris and Lyon, 1860. *Offprint. Freimann, page 224.*

HORKHEIMER, MAX. Die Juden und Europa. Autoritärer Staat. Vernunft & Selbsterhaltung. 1939–1941. Amsterdam, 1968.

SHULVASS, MOSES A. From East to West. The Westward Migration of Jews from Eastern Europe during the Seventeenth and Eighteenth Centuries. Detroit, 1971.

CANADA

KATTAN, NAÏM (editor) Juifs et Canadiens. Montréal, 1967.

KATTAN, NAÏM (editor) Les Juifs et la Communauté Française. Montréal, 1965.

LATIN AMERICA

ITALIAANDER, ROLF. Juden in Lateinamerika. Tel Aviv, 1971.

NORTH AFRICA

BÉNECH, JOSÉ. Un des Aspects du Judaisme. Essai d'explication d'un Mellah (Ghetto marocain) (Kaiserslautern) no date [after 1940]

BENSIMON-DONATH, DORIS. Évolution du Judaïsme Marocain sous le Protectorat français 1912–1956. Paris and La Haye, 1968.

FAITLOVITCH, JACOB. Igereth mevasser. Roma (1935) *Printed in Ethiopic type.*

HALÉVY, J. Prières des Falashas ou Juifs d'Abyssinie. Texte Ethiopien . . . Paris, 1877.

STERN, HENRY A. Wanderings among the Falashas in Abyssinia; together with a Description of the Country and its Various Inhabitants. London, 1862.

ASIA

ABRAHAM, I. S. The Origin and History of the Calcutta Jews. Calcutta (1969)

BEN-DASAN, ISAIAH. The Japanese and the Jews. New York and Tokyo, 1972.

[*Cochin*] The Magna Carta of the Jews in Kerala! The Famous Copper-Plates. A cherished relic preserved by the Jewish Community of Cochin. Ernakulam, S. India, 1967.

GOLB, NORMAN. Spertus College of Judaica Yemenite Manuscripts. An Illustrated Catalogue. Chicago, 1972.

(GOZANI, JEAN-PAUL) Lettres edifiantes et curieuscs ecrites des missions etrangeres par quelques Missionnaires de la Compagnie de Jesus. Paris, 1707. VII. *Recueil. Pages 1–40: Letter of Père Gozani on the Jews of Kai-Fong-Fou.*

KLOETZEL, C. Z. "Anjuvanam" Bericht über eine Reise zu den Schwarzen und Weissen Juden in Cochin (Indien) (Dokumenta Judaica Nummer 1) Mukačevo (1938) *Cover has: Z.C.Kloetzel.*

OPPERT, GUSTAV. Ueber die jüdischen Colonïen in Indien Berlin, 1897 *Offprint.*

RATZABY, YEHUDA. The Yemenite Jews. Literature and Studies. Bibliography 1935–1975. Jerusalem, 1976.

STRIZOWER, SCHIFRA. The Children of Israel: the Bene Israel of Bombay. Oxford (1971)

TOBI, YEHUDA. The Jews of Yemen (Bibliography of Jewish History) Jerusalem, 1975.

AUSTRALIA AND NEW ZEALAND

GETZLER, ISRAEL. Neither Toleration nor Favour. The Australian Chapter of Jewish Emancipation. Carlton, Victoria, 1970.

MISCELLANEOUS COUNTRIES

HYMAN, LOUIS. The Jews of Ireland from Earliest Times to the Year 1910. London/Jerusalem, 1972.

JUDAICA GERMANICA I, *to 1850*

ABRAHAM À S. CLARA [pseudonym of HANS ULRICH MEGERLE] Abrahamisches Gehab dich wohl! oder Urlaube, in diesem End-Wercke seiner Schriften . . . Nürnberg and Wien, 1729.

BALDAMUS, IACOBUS CONRADUS. Veritas Christianae religionis ipsis Iudaeorum obtrectationibus confirmata . . . Halae Magdeburgicae, 1718.

Bemerkungen an das unbefangene und aufgeklärte Hamburgische Publikum. Bei Gelegenheit des Criminal-Prozesses gegen die unglückliche Jüdinn Debora Traub. Hamburg, 1793.

[*Breslau*] Treuer Bericht über die letzten Ereignisse in der hiesigen jüdischen Gemeinde. Breslau, 1846.

CARL WILHELM FERDINAND (HERZOG ZU BRAUNSCHWEIG-LÜNEBURG &C) [Verordnung gegen jüdische Hausierhändler mit Band] Braunschweig, 12. Junius, 1789. *Broadside.*

DITMAR, THEODOR JAKOB. Geschichte der Israeliten bis auf den Cyrus, zur Ehre und Vertheidigung der Bibel und zur Berichtigung des Wolfenbüttelschen Fragmentisten. Berlin, 1788.

[*Dresden*] Vorstellung der Aeltesten der Dresdner Innungen wider die Petition des jüdischen Gemeindevorstandes . . . Dresden (1843)

Erschröckliche Brüderschafft der Alten und Neuen Wiedertäuffer, Quäcker, Schwärmer und Frey-Geister, mit Denen Heil-und Gottlosen Juden . . . No place, 1702.

[DODSLEY, ROBERT] Das Buch Josua, Des Erretters der Sache Der Königin von Ungarn, in dem Krieg der Franzosen . . . aufgeschrieben von Noa Samson dem Ansager der Schule zu Landau. No place, 1745.

[DODSLEY, ROBERT] Die Bücher der Chronick derer Könige von Engelland, beschrieben in der Sprach des Jüdischen Volcks durch Nathan Ben Saddi . . . Franckfurt and Leipzig, 1744.

[DODSLEY, ROBERT] Die Bücher Der Chronicka Friederichs Des Königes der Preussen . . . Beschrieben von Kemuel Saddi, Hof-Juden zu Mannheim. No place, 1744.

[DODSLEY, ROBERT] Die Bücher der Chronicka Carls des Herzogs zu Lothringen . . . Beschrieben in Jüdischer Schreibart von Kemuel Saddi, Hof-Juden zu Mannheim. Franckfurth, 1744.

[DODSLEY, ROBERT] Die Bücher der Chronicka von den Kriegen welche die Frantzosen mit Theresia, der Königin zu Ungarn geführt haben . . . Beschrieben in Jüdischer Schreibart durch Jeckof Ben Saddi . . . Erstes Buch. Prag, 1744. *Not in Muneles.*

[DODSLEY, ROBERT] Chronicka der Königin zu Ungarn und von der Schlacht bey Dettingen; Geschrieben in Jüdischer Schreibart von Abraham Ben Saddi, Hof-Juden in Engelland . . . Franckfurt and Leipzig, 1744.

Effigies monumenti in reproborum Rabinorum et Iudaeorum apostatarum confusionem et ignominiam . . . Rabini Schemhamphoras. Witebergae, 1596. *Broadside with extreme anti-Jewish caricature and poem.*

FRANKEL, Z. Die Eidesleistung der Juden in theologischer und historischer Beziehung. Dresden and Leipzig, 1840.

GANS, E. Rede bei der Wiedereröffnung der Sitzungen des Vereins für Cultur und Wissenschaft der Juden. Gehalten (Berlin . . . 1821) Hamburg, 1822.

GANS, E. Dritter Bericht, im Verein für Cultur und Wissenschaft der Juden, abgestattet . . . 1823. Hamburg, 1823.

HILLER, JOH. WOLFGANG. Demonstratio juridica, veridica, Das die List und betriegliche Griffe, So theils Juden in Bemäntlung ihres Wuchers . . . gebrauchen . . . Noribergae, 1658.

HOLDHEIM, SAM. Ueber Auflösbarkeit der Eide. Von S. L. Rappoport beleuchtet. Hamburg, 1845.

HOLL, FRANCISCUS XAVERIUS. Harmonia juris naturae, canonici, civilis, & publici Germaniae circa educationem liberorum in casu, quo uxor Hebraea, reluctante marito, ad Christiana sacra transiit. Heidelbergae, 1782.

HOSMANN, SIGISMUND. Fürtreffliches Denck-Mahl Der Göttlichen Regierung, Bewiesen an der . . . Güldenen Tafel, und anderer Kostbarciten . . . Cell and Leipzig, 1718.

KLEY, E. Religiöse Lieder und Gesänge für Jisraeliten, zum Gebrauch häuslicher und öffentlicher Gottes-Verehrung. Hamburg, 1818.

KOREFF, DAVID FERDINAND. Du triomphe inévitable et prochain des principes constitutionnels en Prusse . . . Paris, 1821.

[*Koreff*] CANCELLIERI, FRANCESCO. Lettera . . . al Ch. Sig. Dottore Koreff . . . sopra il Tarantismo . . . Roma, 1817.

[*Koreff*] MARTIN, MARIETTA. Le Docteur Koreff (1783–1851) Paris, 1925.

[*Koreff*] OPPELN-BRONIKOWSKI, FRIEDRICH V. (editor) David Ferdinand Koreff Serapionsbruder, Magnetiseur, Geheimrat und Dichter. Der Lebensroman eines Vergessenen . . . Berlin-Leipzig, 1928.

MAIER (KIRCHENRATH DR.) Ueber den Judeneid. Stuttgart, 1852.

MENDELSSOHN, JOSEPH. Pariser Briefe. 3 volumes. Leipzig, 1841. *See Bulletin des Leo Baeck Instituts, number 42 (1968), page 115, footnote, and volume 46–47 (1969), pages 213–214.*

MÜLLER, JOHANNES. Judaismus oder Jüdenthumb, Das ist Aussführlicher Bericht von des Jüdischen Volckes Unglauben, Blindheit und Verstockung . . . Hamburg, 1644.

MÜLLER, JOHANN CHRISTOPH. Greuel der Falschen Messien, wie auch, Schatz-Kammer des Wahren Messiae Jesu Christi . . . Denen Jüden zur Erkäntnis und Reue, allen rechtschaffenen Christen aber zum Trost ans Licht gegeben. No place, 1702.

[OBEREIT, J. H.] Gamaliels eines philosophischen Juden, Spaziergänge . . . Constantinopel [!] 1780.

Ode, Seiner Majestät . . . Friedrich Wilhelm III. bei Gelegenheit Seiner glorreichen Siege und der Befreiung unserer Stadt . . . gewidmet. Aus dem Hebräischen übersetzt [Glogau ?, no date]

Ordnung und Form eines Juden-Eydes wie solche in der kaiserlichen und des Reichs- Cammergerichts Ordnung fundiret . . . Jever, July 2, 1793. *Manuscript.*

[*Paulli*] Novus in Belgio Judaeorum Rex Oliger Paulli, Multis editis monumentis literarii clarus. Das ist Der Neue Juden-König Oliger Paulli, in Niederland, Durch viele herausgegebene Schrifften bekannt. No place, 1702.

SHACHAR, ISAIAH. The Judensau. A Medieval Anti-Jewish Motif and its History. London, 1974.

[Steckbrief gegen eine jüdische Räuberbande wegen eines Raubüberfalls in Schaumburg im Jahr 1802, herausgegeben von der Fürstlich hessisch-schaumburgischen Regierung] [Schaumburg, 1802]

STEIN, LEOPOLD. Der Eid "more judaico," wie solcher bei den Gerichten der freien Stadt Frankfurt noch in Uebung ist . . . Frankfurt am Main, 1847.

STERN, ITZIG FEITEL (pseudonym of HEINRICH HOLZSCHUHER) Israels Verkehr und Geist . . . Meissen, 1833.

STERN, ITZIG FEITEL (pseudonym of HEINRICH HOLZSCHUHER) Lexikon der jüdischen Geschäfts- und Umgangs-Sprache. Jüdisch deutsch und deutsch jüdisch. Leipzig and Meissen, 1858.

STERN, ITZIG FEITEL (pseudonym of HEINRICH HOLZSCHUHER) Die Manzepaziuhn der houchlöbliche kieniglich bayerische Jüdenschaft (Schriften 9. Theil) Leipzig, Meissen and Riesa (1834)

SUSANIS, MARQUARDUS DE. De Iudaeis et usuris tractatus practicus . . . Francofurti, 1613.

[Teuthorn, H. E.] Briefe eines reisenden Juden über den gegenwärtigen Zustand des Religionswesens unter den Protestanten und Catholicken, und über die Auferstehung Jesu. No place, 1781.

Trier, Salomon Abraham (editor) Rabbinische Gutachten über die Beschneidung. Frankfurt am Main, 1844.

Wolanski, (Landrath) v. Rede . . . bei Gelegenheit der durch die israelitische Gemeine zu Inowraclaw, Behufs Einführung ihrer Repräsentanten . . . 1834 veranstalteten Feier. Thorn, 1859.

Wolfart, Ioannes Henricus. Tractatio iuridica de iuramentis Iudaeorum . . . Francofurti and Lipsiae, 1748.

Zunz, L. Gutachten über die Beschneidung. Frankfurt am Main, 1844.

JUDAICA GERMANICA II, *from 1851*

Antisemitismus in Westdeutschland. Eine Dokumentation des Verbandes der Jüdischen Gemeinden in der Deutschen Demokratischen Republik. Berlin, 1967.

[*Baeck, Leo*] Altmann, Alexander. Leo Baeck and the Jewish Mystical Tradition. New York, 1973.

[*Baeck, Leo*] Reichmann, Eva G. (editor) Worte des Gedenkens für Leo Baeck. Heidelberg, 1959.

[*Leo Baeck Institute*] Publications of the Leo Baeck Institute. Year Book 1-current. London, 1970–1972.

Bamberger, Ludwig. Monopol und Sozialismus. Reichstagsrede. Berlin, 1886.

Bamberger, Ludwig. Die Stitchworte der Silberleute. Berlin, 1893. *Third edition.*

Bamberger, Ludwig. Die Stitchworte der Silberleute. Berlin, 1893. *Fourth revised and enlarged edition.*

Bericht der Justiz-Kommission über den Entwurf eines Gesetzes, betreffend die Eide der Juden. Berlin, 1861.

[*Bernays*] Bach, Hans I. Jacob Bernays. Ein Beitrag zur Emanzipationsgeschichte der Juden und zur Geschichte des deutschen Geistes im neunzehnten Jahrhundert. Tübingen, 1974.

Bernstein, A. Die Jahre des Volkes. Geschichtliche Skizzen. Berlin, 1875.

[*Bleichröder*] [Perrot, Fr. Fürchtegott] Die Aera Bleichröder-Delbrück-Camphausen. Berlin, 1876. *Offprint.*

Born, Hedwig and Born, Max. Der Luxus des Gewissens. Erlebnisse und Einsichten im Atomzeitalter. München, 1969.

[*Born, Julius von*] Weisse, S. [Rabbi, and others] Gedächtniss-Feier für den verewigten Vorsitzenden des Verwaltungsraths der Berliner Handels-Gesellschaft Herrn Baron Julius von Born . . . 1897 . . . (Berlin, 1897)

Borries, Hans-Joachim v. Deutschtum und Judentum. Studien zum Selbstverständnis des deutschen Judentums 1879/80. Hamburg, 1971. *Dissertation.*

David, Annie. Von den Juden in Deutschland, 1600–1870. Ein Bildbericht. Jerusalem, 1973.

Davidovicz, David. Wandmalereien in alten Synagogen. Das Wirken des Malers Elieser Sussmann in Deutschland. Hameln-Hannover, 1969.

[*Deutsch, Hans*] Emmenegger, Kurt. Der Fall Deutsch. Tatsachen zu einem Justizskandal. New Haven (Connecticut) and Zürich, 1970.

Elyashiv, Vera. Deutschland – kein Wintermärchen. Eine Israeli sieht die Bundesrepublik. Wien and Düsseldorf, 1964.

Fechenbach, Hermann. Die letzten Mergentheimer Juden und Dic Geschichte der Familien Fechenbach. Stuttgart, 1972.

Feuchtwanger, Lion. Ausgefüllter biographischer Fragebogen. Berlin, no date.

[*Frankl, Wilhelm*] Nowarra, Heinz Joachim. The Jew with the Blue Max. Sun Valley, California, 1967.

Freudenthal, Max (editor) Kriegsgedenkbuch der israelitischen Kultusgemeinde Nürnberg. Nürnberg (1921)

Friedmann, Aron. 50 Jahre in Berlin (1878–1928) Berlin, 1929.

Friedmann, Fritz. Was ich erlebte! Memoiren. 2 volumes. Berlin, 1909–1910.

Gay, Peter. The Berlin-Jewish Spirit a Dogma in Search of Some Doubts. New York, 1972.

[*Geiger, Abraham*] Wiener, Max. Abraham Geiger and Liberal Judaism. The Challenge of the Nineteenth Century. Philadelphia, 1962.

Zur Geschichte der Juden in Deutschland im 19. und 20. Jahrhundert. Jerusalem, 1971.

Goldstein-Laczkó, Georgette (editor) Worte des Talmud ausgewählt und eingeleitet von Rabbi Goldstein. Tübingen, 1963.

Gumbel, E. J. Les crimes politiques en Allemagne 1919–1929. Paris, 1931.

HAMBURGER, ERNEST. Jews, Democracy and Weimar Germany. New York, 1973.

HEYMANN, A. H. Lebenserinnerungen (editor, Heinrich Loewe) Berlin, 1909.

[*Hirsch, Maurice de*] SINAY, REUBEN. La coupe d'amertume. Lamentations en mémorie du . . . Baron Moïse de Hirsch qui quitta ce monde . . . 1896. Service commemoratif célébré . . . par les colons de Moiseville, en Republica Argentine . . . Manchester, 1897.

HORKHEIMER, MAX. Über die deutschen Juden. Köln, 1961.

[*Jacoby, Johann*] SILBERNER, EDMUND. Johann Jacoby, Politiker und Mensch. Bonn-Bad Godesberg, 1977.

Juden als Erfinder und Entdecker. Berlin-Wilmersdorf, 1913.

Wo Juden bei Juden wohnen können . . . Berlin, 1937.

JULIUS. In Deutschland 1945–1946. Jerusalem, 1947.

KALIPHARI, SALOMON GEN. POSNER. Mein Lebensbild im Anschluss an sieben Ahnenbilder dargestellt von S. K. gen. P. und aus dem Hebräischen übertragen von seinem Enkelsohne Dr. Moritz Landsberg . . . Breslau, no date. *Lithographed. Freimann, page 50.*

KNÜTTER, HANS-HELMUTH. Die Juden und die deutsche Linke in der Weimarer Republik 1918–1933. Düsseldorf, 1971.

KROHN, HELGA. Die Juden in Hamburg 1800–1850. Ihre soziale, kulturelle und politische Entwicklung während der Emanzipationszeit. Frankfurt am Main, 1967.

LASKER, EDUARD. Wege und Ziele der Culturentwickelung. Leipzig, 1881.

LAZARUS, MORITZ. Lebenserinnerungen. Berlin, 1906.

LEHMANN, J. A. EMIL. Der Deutsche jüdischen Bekenntnisses. Vortrag . . . Berlin, 1894.

LEHMANN, EMIL. Höre Israel! Aufruf an die deutschen Glaubensgenossen. Dresden, 1869.

LINDAU, PAUL. Nur Erinnerungen. 2 volumes. Stuttgart and Berlin, 1919.

[*Loewe*] TISCHERT, GEORG (editor) Aus der Entwicklung des Loewe-Konzerns. Berlin, 1911.

LONSBACH, RICHARD MAXIMILIAN (pseudonym of R. CAHEN] Friedrich Nietzsche und die Juden. Stockholm, 1939. *Wilhelm Sternfeld and Eva Tiedemann, Deutsche Exil-Literatur 1933–1945, page 206.*

MOSSE, GEORGE L. The Jews and the German War Experience 1914–1918 (New York) 1977.

MOSSE, WERNER E. (editor) Entscheidungsjahr 1932. Zur Judenfrage in der Endphase der Weimarer Republik. Tübingen, 1965.

MOSSE, WERNER E. (editor) Deutsches Judentum in Krieg und Revolution 1916–1923. Tübingen, 1971.

[*Nathan, Paul*] FEDER, ERNST. Politik und Humanität. Paul Nathan. Ein Lebensbild. Berlin, 1929.

NEUMEYER, ALFRED. Lichter und Schatten. Eine Jugend in Deutschland. München, 1967.

NIEWYK, DONALD L. Socialist, Anti-Semite, and Jew. German Social Democracy Confronts the Problem of Anti-Semitism 1918–1933. Baton Rouge, 1971.

OPPENHEIMER, FRANZ. Der Arbeitslohn. Kritische Studie. Jena, 1926.

OPPENHEIMER, FRANZ. Die soziale Frage und der Sozialismus. Jena, 1919.

OPPENHEIMER, FRANZ. Gemeineigentum und Privateigentum an Grund und Boden. Berlin (1914)

OPPENHEIMER, FRANZ. Das Grundgesetz der Marxschen Gesellschaftslehre. Jena, 1926.

OPPENHEIMER, FRANZ. Alte und neue Makkabäer. Gedenkrede . . . Berlin, 1906.

OPPENHEIMER, FRANZ. Sozialisierung. No place, no date [about 1919]

OPPENHEIMER, FRANZ. Theorie der reinen und politischen Ökonomie. Berlin, 1919.

OPPENHEIMER, FRANZ. Weder Kapitalismus noch Kommunismus. Stuttgart, 1962.

OPPENHEIMER, FRANZ. Weder so – noch so. Der dritte Weg. Potsdam, 1933.

OPPENHEIMER, FRANZ. Weltwirtschaft und Nationalwirtschaft. Berlin, 1915.

OPPENHEIMER, FRANZ. Wert und Kapitalprofit. Neubegründung der objektiven Wertlehre. Jena, 1916.

PAPPENHEIM, BERTHA. Gebete (Berlin) 1936.

PAPPENHEIM, BERTHA. Allerlei Geschichten (Maasse-Buch) Frankfurt am Main, 1929.

[*Pappenheim, Bertha*] FREEMAN, LUCY. The Story of Anna O. New York, 1972.

Perspectives of German-Jewish History in the 19th and 20th Century. Jerusalem, 1971.

[*Preuss, Hugo*] GRASSMANN, SIEGFRIED. Hugo Preuss und die deutsche Selbstverwaltung. Lübeck and Hamburg, 1965.

ROSENMEYER, LUDWIG. Erinnerungsbilder aus meinem Leben. Frankfurt am Main, 1931.

ROSENTHAL, L. Ernstes und Heiteres aus dem jüdischen Leben. Leipzig, 1921.

SCHMIDT, RUDOLF. Zur Geschichte unserer heimischen jüdischen Gemeinden. Eberswalde, 1929.

[*Schocken*] POPPEL, STEPHEN M. Salman Schocken and the Schocken Verlag: A Jewish Publisher in Weimar and Nazi Germany [Cambridge, Massachusetts] 1973. *Offprint.*

SCHOEPS, HANS-JOACHIM. "Bereit für Deutschland!" Der Patriotismus deutscher Juden und der Nationalsozialismus. Frühe Schriften 1930 bis 1939. Eine historische Dokumentation. Berlin, 1970.

SCHOEPS, HANS-JOACHIM. Rufmord 1970. Beiheft zu "Bereit für Deutschland" . . . (Erlangen and Berlin, 1970)

SCHWABACH, PAUL H. VON. Aus meinen Akten. Berlin, 1927. *Privatdruck.*

SCHWARZ, ADOLF. Grabrede auf den im Duell gefallenen Herrn cand. med. Eduard Salomon . . . 1890. Karlsruhe, 1890.

[*Simmel*] WOLFF, KURT H. (editor) Georg Simmel, 1858–1918. Columbus [Ohio] 1959.

Statistik des Bundes jüdischer Frontsoldaten Dortmund-Hörde (Stadt und Land) Dortmund. no date.

STERN, HEINEMANN. Warum hassen sie uns eigentlich? Jüdisches Leben zwischen den Kriegen. Erinnerungen (editor, Hans Ch. Meyer) Düsseldorf, 1970.

STERN, SELMA. Josel of Rosheim, Commander of Jewry in the Holy Roman Empire of the German Nation. Philadelphia, 1965.

[*Tietz*] 50 Jahre Leonhard Tietz 1879/1929. Köln, 1929.

[*Tucholsky*] RADDATZ, FRITZ, J. Tucholsky. Eine Bildbiographie. München, 1961.

ULLSTEIN, HEINZ. Spielplatz meines Lebens. Erinnerungen. München, 1961.

[*Wassermann, Jakob*] BLANKENAGEL, JOHN C. The Writings of Jakob Wassermann. Boston, 1942.

[*Wassermann, Jakob*] KARLWEIS, MARTA (MARTA WASSERMANN) Jakob Wassermann. Bild, Kampf und Werk. Amsterdam, 1935.

[*Wassermann, Jakob*] SZILÁGYI, ERNÖ. Wassermann zsidó önvallomása ("Mein Weg als Deutscher und Jude") [Also] WASSERMANN, JACOB. A fürthi messiás. Kolozsvar, 1943.

WENZEL, STEFI. Jüdische Bürger und kommunale Selbstverwaltung in preussischen Städten 1808–1848. Berlin, 1967.

WILLSTÄTTER, RICHARD. Aus meinem Leben. Von Arbeit, Musse und Freunden. Weinheim/Bergstr., 1958.

Die Wirksamkeit des von der Grossloge für Deutschland U.O.B.B. ernannten Comitees zur Bekämpfung des Mädchenhandels. Hamburg, 1900.

Jüdisches (U.O.B.B.) Zweigkomitee des Deutschen National-Komitees zur Bekämpfung des Mädchenhandels. Galizische Abordnung. Bericht der Sendbotin (Lemberg, 1906)

JUDAICA GERMANICA III

AUERBACH, BARUCH. Gebet und Festgesang für Seine Majestät den König Wilhelm und für Ihre Majestät die Königin Marie Luise Augusta. Berlin, 1861.

BACH, JOSEPH. Worte . . . bei der von der Israeliten-Gemeinde zu Pesth . . . 1835 abgehaltenen Gedächtniss-Feier Sr. Höchstseligen Majestät . . . Kaisers und Königs Franz I. Pesth (1835)

CAHN, M. 20 Gebete in Veranlassung der Geburtstagsfeier Sr. Majestät des Kaisers und Königs und einiger patriotischer Gedenktage. No place [Fulda ?] no date.

COHN, F. Die Sprache eines Denkmals. Predigt zur Jahresfeier des Frankfurter Friedensschlusses . . . 1873 . . . zu Oels gehalten [Oels, 1873]

HIRSCH, AARON. Regenbogen. Eine Andachtsrede zu Ehren der . . . Seele unsers . . . Königs und Landesvaters Friedrich Wilhelm III. und des Thronfolgers . . . Sr. Erlauchten Majestät Friedrich Wilhelm IV. Königs von Preussen. Krotoschin . . . 1840. Breslau (1840?)

JAPHET, L. Sieg und Frieden. Zwei religiöse Vorträge gehalten . . . zum vierundsiebenzigsten Geburtstage Sr. Majestät des Kaisers und Königs Wilhelm I. . . . 1871 . . . Goslar, 1871.

JOSEPH (RABBINER) Leichenrede des Herzogs Maximilian Julius Leopold von Braunschweig Hochfürstl. Durchl. Frankfurt an der Oder, 1785.

KOHN, J. Drei Thränen. Predigt aus Veranlassung der Erkrankung Sr. Kaiserl. Hoheit des deutschen Kronprinzen gehalten . . . 1887 . . . zu Inowrazlaw. Inowrazlaw (1887)

PLESSNER, SALOMON. Der lehrreiche Moment oder: Das erhabene Werkzeug in Gottes Händen. Rede, bei Gelegenheit der . . . Dankfeier für die Erhaltung Sr. Königlichen Majestät . . . Posen, 1844.

ROSENBERG, JACOB. Gedächtnisspredigt zum Andenken Sr. Hochseligen Majestät des Königs Friedrich Wilhelm III., gehalten . . . 1840 . . . zu Düsseldorf. Düsseldorf, 1840.

SCHREIBER, EMANUEL. Die irdische Majestät gleicht der himmlischen. Festpredigt . . . am Geburtstage Sr. Majestät des Kaisers. Elbing, 1876.

TAUBER, JACOB. Das vierzigste Offenbarungsfest unter der Regierung Sr. Majestät Franz Josef I. Rede . . . Prerau, 1888.

EMANCIPATION IN GERMANY AND AUSTRIA I

[*Bauer, Bruno*] HIRSCH, SAMUEL. Das Judenthum, der christliche Staat und die moderne Kritik. Briefe zur Beleuchtung der Judenfrage von Bruno Bauer. Leipzig, 1843.

[GRATTENAUER, KARL WILHELM FRIEDRICH] Wider die Juden. Ein Wort der Warnung an alle unsere christliche Mitbürger. Berlin, 1803. *Second edition. Eichstädt, 368.*

HEILBUT, A. Fragen und Bemerkungen veranlasst durch die Schrift des Herrn Carl Valentiner, . . . "Ueber die Aufnahme der Juden in den christlichen Staat." Altona, 1841.

HUNDT-RADOWSKY, HARTWIG VON. Truthähnchen. Ein satyrisch-komischer Roman. Merseburg, 1820.

ITZENPLITZ (GRAF VON) Gutachten der Abtheilung der Herren-Kurie zur Berathung über eine Verordnung zur Feststellung der Verhältnisse der Juden in den Königlich Preussischen Staaten (Berlin, 1847)

JACOBY, JOHANN. Beschränkung der Redefreiheit. Eine Provocation auf rechtliches Gehör. Mannheim, 1846.

[JACOBY, JOHANN] Vier Fragen, beantwortet von einem Ostpreussen. Mannheim, 1841.

Bibliothek Dr. Joh. Jacoby. Königsberg im Preussen, 1882. *Sales catalogue.*

[*Jacoby, Johann*] BRASCH, MORITZ. Philosophie und Politik. Studien über Ferd. Lassalle und Johann Jacoby. Leipzig, no date [1889]

KLÜBER, J. S. Historische und staatsrechtliche Lösung der beiden europäischen Lebensfragen: über die natürlichsten Mittel der Juden-Emancipation . . . Erlangen, 1838. *Eichstädt, 1041.*

Die Landtagsverhandlungen über die bürgerliche Stellung der Juden in Preussen. Mit Beziehung auf Oesterreich. Leipzig, 1847. *Eichstädt, 1933.*

EMANCIPATION IN GERMANY AND AUSTRIA II

KATZ, JACOB. Emancipation and Assimilation. Studies in Modern Jewish History (London) 1972.

NIELSEN, FREDRIK. Den moderne Jødedom. En Kritik og en Karakteristik. Kjøbenhavn, 1879.

TOURY, JACOB. Der Eintritt der Juden ins deutsche Bürgertum. Eine Dokumentation. Tel Aviv, 1972.

TOURY, JACOB. Eine vergessene Frühschrift zur Emanzipation der Juden in Deutschland. Tel-Aviv, 1969. *Offprint.*

FRANKFORT

Erneuerter Abdruck eines Gutachtens der Juristen-Facultät auf der . . . Universität zu Giesen, Die Vertheidigung der Anmassung der Frankfurter Juden-Gemeinde auf das Bürger-Recht der freyen Stadt Frankfurt betreffend. No place, 1817.

ARNSBERG, PAUL. Bilder aus dem jüdischen Leben im alten Frankfurt. Frankfurt am Main, 1970.

[*Fettmilch Riots*] JONAS, JUSTUS VON WAHRNRECHTIGEN. Tricinium. I. Cursum Francofordianum. II. Cursum Mundi . . . No place, 1616.

[*Fettmilch Riots*] STOLTZE, ADOLF. Vinzenz Fettmilch. Drama in fünf Aufzügen. Frankfurt am Main, 1927.

HOROVITZ, M. Jüdische Aerzte in Frankfurt a.M. Frankfurt am Main, 1886.

HOROVITZ, M. Frankfurter Rabbinen. 4 volumes in 1. Frankfurt am Main, 1882–1885.

KRACAUER, I. (editor) Urkundenbuch zur Geschichte der Juden in Frankfurt am Main von 1150–1400. 2 volumes in 1. Frankfurt am Main, 1914. *Supersedes erroneous previous entry in Katalog Judaica, volume I, page 206.*

MERTON, RICHARD. Erinnerswertes aus meinem Leben das über das Persönliche hinausgeht. Frankfurt am Main, 1955.

[*Merton*] Wilhelm Merton und sein soziales Vermächtnis. Gedenkworte . . . anlässlich der zehnten Wiederkehr seines Todestages. Frankfurt am Main, 1926.

Fünfzig Jahre Metallgesellschaft 1881–1931. Denkschrift bearbeitet von Dr. Walther Däbritz. Frankfurt am Main, 1931.

Mitteilungen der Gesellschaft zur Erforschung jüdischer Kunstdenkmäler zu Frankfurt am Main. Volume I–II. Frankfurt am Main, 1900–1901.

Statuten der Gesellschaft zur Erforschung jüdischer Kunstdenkmäler in Frankfurt a.M. Frankfurt am Main, 1897.

[*Schiff*] ARNSBERG, PAUL. Jakob H. Schiff. Von der Frankfurter Judengasse zur Wallstreet. Frankfurt am Main, 1969.

Neue Stättigkeits- und Schutz-Ordnung der Judenschaft zu Frankfurt am Main, deren Verfassung, Verwaltung, Rechte und Verbindlichkeiten betreffend . . . Frankfurt am Main, 1808. *Eichstädt, 498.*

BAVARIA ~~I to 1850~~

100 Jahre Bankhaus H. Aufhäuser (München, 1970)

FREIMANN, A. Aus der Geschichte der Juden in Regensburg von der Mitte des 15. Jahrhunderts bis zur Vertreibung im Jahre 1519. Breslau, 1916. *Offprint.*

GANZENMÜLLER, EUGEN. Ichenhausen. Vom Dorf zum Markt zur Stadt. Ichenhausen, 1970. *Pages 153–172.*

GOLDSCHMIDT, J. D. Ein Wort über die israelitischen Glaubensgenossen zur allgemeinen Beherzigung. München, 1822.

PERLES, JOSEPH. Antrittspredigt gehalten . . . 1871. München, 1871.

[*Perles*] Worte der Erinnerung an den . . . 1894 aus dem Leben geschiedenen Rabbiner . . . Dr. Josef Perles. München (1894)

SINZ, HEINRICH. Ergänzungen zur Geschichte von Ichenhausen und Umgebung. Ichenhausen, 1955.

STERN, MORITZ. Der Regensburger Judenprozess 1476–1480. Berlin [1935]

WERNER, C. Antrittspredigt, gehalten . . . 1895. München, 1895.

BAVARIA II *from 1851*

KIRSCHNER, MAX. Die Sterblichkeit und die Todesursachen der Juden in München von 1881 bis 1908. München, 1912. *Dissertation.*

PERLES, JOSEPH. Predigt zur fünfzigjährigen Jubelfeier der Synagoge zu München . . . 1876. München, 1876.

SZULWAS, MOSES. Die Juden in Würzburg während des Mittelalters. Berlin, 1934.

By MOSES MENDELSSOHN

MENDELSSOHN, MOSES. Denkmal der Freundschaft. Stammbuchblätter und Widmungen (editor, Fritz Bamberger) Berlin, 1929. *Meyer, 53.*

MENDELSSOHN, MOSES. Phädon oder über die Unsterblichkeit der Seele, in drey Gesprächen. Frankfurt and Leipzig, 1778. *Meyer, 146.*

MENDELSSOHN, MOSES. Ueber die Empfindungen. Berlin, 1756. *This edition not in Meyer.*

MENDELSSOHN, MOSES. An die Freunde Lessings. Ofen, 1821. *Elfter Band of Sämmtliche Werke. Meyer, 62.*

MENDELSSOHN, MOSES. Jerusalem oder über religiöse Macht und Judenthum. Ofen, 1819. *Fünfter Band of Sämmtliche Werke. Meyer, 62.*

MENDELSSOHN, MOSES. Phädon oder über die Unsterblichkeit der Seele. Leipzig (Reclam) no date. *This 154 page edition not in Meyer.*

MENDELSSOHN, MOSES. Morgenstunden oder Vorlesungen über das Daseyn Gottes. Erster Theil. Berlin, 1785. *All published. First edition. Meyer, 323.*

MENDELSSOHN, MOSES. Morgenstunden oder Vorlesungen über das Daseyn Gottes. Erster Theil. Ofen and Gross-Wardein, 1819. *All published. Sechster Band of Sämmtliche Werke. Meyer, 62.*

MENDELSSOHN, MOSES. Phädon oder über die Unsterblichkeit der Seele, in drey Gesprächen. Reutlingen, 1789. *Meyer, 151.*

MENDELSSOHN, MOSES. Phädon oder über die Unsterblichkeit der Seele. Ofen, 1819. *erster Band of Sämmtliche Werke. Meyer, 62.*

MENDELSZOON, MOSES. Phedon of over de Onsterflykheid der Ziele, in drie T'zamenspraaken . . . 's Graavenhaage, 1769. *Meyer, 180.*

MENDELSZOON, MOSES. Phedon of over de Onsterflykheid der Ziele, in drie T'zamenspraaken . . . 's Graavenhaage, 1776. *Meyer, 181.*

MENDELSSOHN, MOSES. Die Psalmen. Ofen and Gross-Wardein, 1819. *Achter Band of Sämmtliche Werke. Meyer, 62.*

MENDELSSOHN, MOSES. Ritualgesetze der Juden, betreffend Erbschaften, Vormundschaftssachen, Testamente und Ehesachen, in so weit sie das Mein und Dein angehen. Berlin, 1799. *Fourth edition. Meyer, 240.*

MENDELSSOHN, MOSES. Ritualgesetze der Juden, betreffend Erbschaften, Vormundschaften, Testamente und Ehesachen, in so weit sie das Mein und Dein angehen. Ofen and Gross-Wardein, 1819. *Siebenter Band of Sämmtliche Werke. Meyer, 62.*

MANASSEH BEN ISRAEL. De Verlossing der Jooden . . . met een Voorreden verrykt door Moses Mendelssohn . . . s'Gravenhage, 1782. *Meyer, 270.*

MANASSEH BEN ISRAEL. Rettung der Juden. Aus dem Englischen übersetzt. Nebst einer Vorrede von Moses Mendelssohn. Berlin and Stettin, 1782. *Meyer, 262.*

MENDELSSOHN-LAVATER CONTROVERSY

MENDELSSOHN, MOSES. Schreiben an den Herrn Diaconus Lavater zu Zürich. London, 1770. *Meyer, 200.*

On MOSES MENDELSSOHN

ALTMANN, ALEXANDER. Moses Mendelssohn, a biographical study. Philadelphia, 1973.

FREUND, S. Gedächtniss-Rede am hundertjährigen Todestage Moses Mendelssohn's . . . 1886. Görlitz, 1886. *Not in Meyer.*

GOLDSCHMIDT, A. M. Festrede bei der . . . Gedächtnissfeier Moses Mendelssohn's. Leipzig, 1861. *Meyer, 838.*

HORWITZ, L. Jüdische Familiennamen in der Heimat Mendelssohns. Dessau, 1931. *Offprint.*

ROTH, HELGA INGEBORG GERTRUD. Untersuchungen über Moses Mendelssohns religionsphilosophische Problematik. Bonn, no date. *Dissertation.*

SILBERSTEIN, M. Ein Jünger Moses Mendelssohns. Rede bei der Beerdigung des . . . Landrabbiner Dr. L. Adler . . . 1886. Cassel, 1886.

SOMERHAUSEN, H. Redevoering inhoudende eene korte Levensbeschrijving en den Lof van Moses Mendelszoon . . . Amsterdam, 1812. *Meyer, 777.*

WOLFF, ALFRED. Der Toleranzgedanke in der deutschen Literatur zur Zeit Mendelssohns. Berlin, 1915. *Meyer, 1040.*

ZAREK, OTTO. Moses Mendelssohn. Budapest [about 1936] *Hungarian. Not in Meyer.*

MENDELSSOHN FAMILY

GILBERT, FELIX (editor) Bankiers, Künstler und Gelehrte. Unveröffentlichte Briefe der Familie Mendelssohn aus dem 19. Jahrhundert. Tübingen, 1975.

[*Mendelssohn-Bartholdy*] BARTELS, BERNHARD. Mendelssohn-Bartholdy. Mensch und Werk. Bremen and Hannover, 1947.

[*Mendelssohn-Bartholdy*] Felix Mendelssohn Bartholdy. Bodleian Library, Oxford, 1972. *Exhibition catalogue.*

[*Mendelssohn-Bartholdy*] Felix Mendelssohn Bartholdy. Dokumente seines Lebens. Ausstellung zum 125. Todestag . . . Berlin-Dahlem, 1972. *Exhibition catalogue.*

[*Mendelssohn-Bartholdy*] Endreim-Spiele mit Felix Mendelssohn. Weimar, November 1821. Berlin and Basel, 1970.

[*Mendelssohn, Dorothea*] SCHLEGEL, DOROTHEA VON. Autograph Letter Signed, 1½ pages [Frankfurt am Main] December 27 [18]31, To Elisabeth Malss, sending wine out of Christian religious motivations. Additional note, 1½ pages. No date. Mentioning her son Philipp [Veit] *See Stargardt Katalog 599.*

MENDELSSOHN CIRCLE

BENDAVID, L[AZARUS] Autograph Letter Signed, 1 page. Berlin, November 16 [18]15. Attests that the boys Samuel Is. Seemann and Wolf Lesser attend the Jüdische Freischule and are as worthy as needy of support.

KOREFF, DAVID FERDINAND. Du triomphe inévitable et prochain des principes constitutionnels en Prusse . . . Paris, 1821.

VOIGT (PROFESSOR) Sendschreiben an Hrn. David Friedländer in Berlin, über seinen Beitrag zur Geschichte der Verfolgung der Juden im 19ten Jahrhundert durch Schriftsteller. Königsberg, 1820.

FRIEDLAENDER'S SENDSCHREIBEN

[HERMES, HERMANN DANIEL] Ueber das Sendschreiben einiger Hausväter jüdischer Religion an den Herrn Oberconsistorialrath Teller und die von demselben darauf ertheilte Antwort. Leipzig, 1799. *Littmann, 13; Eichstädt, 348.*

PAALZOW, CHRISTIAN LUDWIG. Die Juden. Nebst einigen Bemerkungen über das Sendschreiben an . . . Probst Teller zu Berlin von einigen Hausvätern jüdischer Religion und die darauf erfolgte Tellersche Antwort. Berlin, 1799. *Littmann, 10; Eichstädt, 343.*

SALOMON MAIMON

MAIMON, SALOMON. Streifereien im Gebiete der Philosophie. Erster Theil. Berlin, 1793. *All published.*

FRIEDENTHAL, HERBERT. The Everlasting Nay. The Death of Salomon Maimon. London, 1944.

LESSING'S NATHAN

LESSING, EFRAIMO. Natano il Saggio. Poema Drammatico. Firenze, 1882.

(DEZIUS, HUGO) Lessing's Nathan der Weise auf der Berliner Bühne. Berlin, 1843.

GEHRKE, HANS. Lessings "Nathan der Weise" Biographie und Interpretation. Hollfeld, 1974.

JUD SUESS

Umständlicher Bericht von der Execution des Juden Süss Oppenheimers . . . Freyburg (1738)

Wahrer Bericht von den Letzten Stunden des Welt-bekandten Juden, Joseph Süss Oppenheimer . . . Freyburg [1738]

Fortsetzung des Wahren Berichts von der Aufführung des Juden, Joseph Süss Oppenheimer, in den letzten Tagen seines Lebens gegen die zu ihm ins Gefängniss geschickte Herren Geistlichen. Freyburg, 1738.

Bernard, Christoph David. Ausführlicher Discurs mit Einem seiner guten Freunde, Von Allem, Was Ihme in den drey letzten Tagen des unglücklichen Jud Süss Oppenheimers . . . bekannt worden. . . . Tübingen, 1738. *Freimann, page 283.*

Feuchtwanger, Lion. Jew Suess. London, 1926.

Feuchtwanger, Lion. Jøden Süss. København, 1928.

Feuchtwanger, Lion. Süss, l'ebreo. Milano, 1930.

Hauff, Wilhelm. Jud Süss. Erzählung. Wiesbaden, 1917.

FRIEDRICH JULIUS STAHL

Stahl, Friedrich Julius. Geschichte der Rechtsphilosophie. Heidelberg, 1847.

Stahl, Federico Giulio. Storia della filosofia del diritto. Torino, 1853.

Kropatscheck, Gerhard. Friedrich Julius Stahl (1802–1861) Vortrag . . . Berlin, 1911.

GABRIEL RIESSER

Deutsch, G. Gabriel Riesser. No place, 1906.

Rosenberg (Dr.) Gabriel Riesser. Festrede . . . (Thorn, no date)

[Weil, Jacob] Sendschreiben an Herrn Dr. Gabriel Riesser in Hamburg. Frankfurt am Main, 1832. *Eichstädt, 904.*

By HEINRICH HEINE

Heine, Henri. Allemands et Français. Paris, 1868. *Wilhelm, I/1195.*

Heine, Heinrich. Buch der Lieder. Mit 15 Gelatineradierungen von Josef Eberz. München, 1923. *Limited Edition. Wilhelm, I/389.*

Heine, Enrico. Confessioni. Lanciano (1923) *Wilhelm, I/1490.*

Heine, Heinrich. It will be a Lovely Day. Selections from the Prose Works. Berlin, 1965. *Seifert, Heine-Bibliographie 1954–1964, 234a.*

Heine, Enrico. Divagazioni musicali. Torino, 1928.

Heine, Enrico. Germania. Lanciano, 1917. *Wilhelm, I/1430 and 1486.*

Heine, Enrico. Che cosa è la Germania. Analisi e profezie. Milano (1915) *Wilhelm, I/1488.*

Heine, Enrico Idillio Alpino (dalla Harzreise) Imola, 1922. *Wilhelm, I/1531.*

Heine, Enrico. L'Intermezzo. Imola, 1880. *Wilhelm, I/1502.*

Heine, Enrico. Leggende e poesie. Milano, 1885. *Wilhelm, I/1425.*

Heine, Enrico Il mare del Nord. Firenze, 1920. *Wilhelm, I/1521.*

Heine, Enrico. Nani, elfi e salamandri. Milano [1922] *Wilhelm, I/1458.*

Heine, Enrico. Della Polonia. Memorie. Milano, 1915. *Wilhelm, I/1523.*

Heine, Enrico. Quando eravamo studenti. Milano, no date.

Heine, Heinrich. Der Rabbi von Bacherach. Mit Originallithographien von Max Liebermann. Berlin, 1923. *Wilhelm, I/545. Limited, numbered, autographed edition.*

Heine, Heinrich. Der Rabbi von Bacherach. Berlin, 1937. *Wilhelm, I/547.*

Heine, Henri. Reisebilder. Tableaux de voyages. 2 volumes. Paris, no date. *Wilhelm, I/1187 and 1288.*

Heine, Henri. Reisebilder. Tableaux de voyage. Paris, 1867. *Wilhelm, I/1288, another edition.*

Heine, Enrico. Reisebilder (Figurine di viaggio) 2 volumes. Ancona, 1912; Milano, 1914. *Wilhelm, I/1533.*

Heine [Henri] Le Tambour Le Grand [Porrentruy] 1944. *Wilhelm, I/1263.*

Heine, Henrik. Válogatott költeményei (editor, Spóner Andor) Budapest, 1906. *Wilhelm, I/1955.*

Heinebuch. Eine Auswahl aus Heinrich Heines Dichtungen (editor, Otto Ernst) Hamburg-Grossborstel, 1906. *Wilhelm, I/148.*

Heine-Lesebuch. Poesie und Prosa (editor, H. Werneke) Kehl (Baden) 1931. *Wilhelm, I/169.*

Kloos, Willem (editor) Heinrich Heine als Dichter. Bloemlezing . . . Amsterdam, 1906. *Wilhelm, I/149.*

On HEINRICH HEINE

Bruns, Friedrich (editor) Die Lese der deutschen Lyrik von Klopstock bis Rilke. New York, no date. *See statistic on page 60.*

BURGER, LUDWIG. Heine's Memoiren. Fantastische Oper . . . Text mit Verwendung mehrerer Gedichte von Heine von Eduard v. Dubsky [Pressburg, 1891] *Wilhelm*, II/*3987*.

CARNIOL, FRIEDRICH. Heinrich Heine, ein Requiem. Zum Todestage. Leipzig, 1909. *In: Xenien, Jahrgang 1909, Heft Nummer 2. Wilhelm,* II/*550*.

CHANDLER, STÉPHANIE. Henri Heine. Essai anthologique. Bruxelles, 1940. *Limited numbered edition. Presentation copy. Wilhelm,* II/*141*.

DEBLUË-BERNSTEIN, VERA. Anima naturaliter ironica – Die Ironie in Wesen und Werk Heinrich Heines. Bern, 1970. *Dissertation.*

Dichterliebe. Heinrich Heine im Lied. Ein Verzeichnis der Vertonungen von Gedichten Heinrich Heines zusammengestellt zum 175. Geburtstag des Dichters. Hamburg, 1972.

DRESCH, JOSEPH. Heine à Paris (1831–1856) d'après sa correspondance et les témoignages de ses contemporains. Paris, 1956. *Seifert, 1200.*

DUCROS, LOUIS. Henri Heine et son temps (1799–1827) Paris, 1886. *Wilhelm,* II/*95*.

(DUDDA, JOHANNES) Heinrich Heine. Leben und Werk. Weimar, 1973.

EMBDEN, LUDWIG VON. The Family Life of Heinrich Heine . . . London, 1893. *Wilhelm,* II/*1323 but translated by Charles Godfrey Leland.*

EULENBERG, HERBERT. Heinrich Heine. Berlin, 1947. *Wilhelm,* II/*342*.

FEUCHTWANGER, LION. Heinrich Heines "Rabbi von Bacherach." München, 1907. *Wilhelm,* II/*3103*.

GNAD, ERNST. Ueber den Charakter der Heine'schen Dichtung. Triest, 1870. *In: "Populäre Vorträge über Dichter und Dichtkunst." Wilhelm,* II/*211*.

GROTTHUSS, JEANNOT EMIL FRHR. VON. Heinrich Heine als deutscher Lyriker. Eine litterarische Ketzerei. Stuttgart, 1894. *Wilhelm,* II/*2662*.

HALUSA, TEZELIN. Heinrich Heine. In charakteristischen Zügen zum 100. Geburtstag entworfen. München and Wien, 1899. *Wilhelm,* II/*457*.

Heine Gedenktage, Erinnerungen und Geburtstags-Buch. Berlin, etc. [1913] *Wilhelm,* I/*71*.

Heine-Jahrbuch 1962–1971. Herausgegeben vom Heine-Archiv Düsseldorf. 10 volumes. Hamburg, 1961–1971.

Heine-Jahrbuch 1962–1973. Herausgegeben vom Heine-Archiv (ab 1973: Heinrich-Heine-Institut) Düsseldorf. 12 volumes. Hamburg, 1961–1973.

Heine-Kalender für das Jahr 1910, 1911, 1912 (editor, Eugen Korn) 3 volumes. Berlin-Leipzig, 1909–1911. *Wilhelm,* II/*75*.

HEINE, MARIA EMBDEN. Ricordi della vita intima di Enrico Heine per sua nipote M.E.H. (Principessa della Rocca) Firenze, 1880. *Wilhelm,* II/*92*.

ILBERG, WERNER. Unser Heine. Eine kritische Würdigung. Berlin, 1952. *Wilhelm,* II/*151*.

Illustrationen zu Heinrich Heine. Leipzig, 1972.

JÖRGENSEN, ALF. Karl Kraus. Der Heinefresser und die Ursachen. Eine Studie über moderne Journalistik. Flensburg [1912] *Wilhelm,* II/*3409*.

KAUFMANN, MAX. Heines Charakter und die moderne Seele. Zürich, 1902. *Wilhelm,* II/*1271*.

KREUTZER, LEO. Heine und der Kommunismus. Göttingen, 1970.

KRUSE, JOSEPH A. Heines Hamburger Zeit (Heine-Studien, editor Manfred Windfuhr) Hamburg, 1972.

KURZ, PAUL KONRAD. Künstler Tribun Apostel. Heinrich Heine's Auffassung vom Beruf des Dichters. München, 1967.

MEISSNER, ALFRED. Heinrich Heine. Erinnerungen. Amsterdam, 1856. *Wilhelm,* II/*1727*.

MENDE, FRITZ. Heinrich Heine. Chronik seines Lebens und Werkes. Berlin, 1970.

MEYER-BENFEY, HEINRICH. Heinrich Heine. Der Dichter des Buchs der Lieder. Neue Heine-Litteratur. Berlin, 1907. *Wilhelm,* II/*2927*.

MIRECOURT, EUGÈNE DE [pseudonym of CH. J. B. JACQUOT] Henri Heine (Les Contemporains) Paris, 1871. *Wilhelm,* II/*198*.

NEANDER, MAXIMILIAN. Deutschland Ein Wintermärchen nach Heinrich Heine. Berlin, 1920. *Wilhelm,* II/*3940*.

NORD, H. Heinrich Heine als Dichter, Mensch und Deutscher. Hamburg [1910] *Wilhelm,* II/*556*.

NOVÁK, ARNE. Menzel, Boerne, Heine. Studie literárně-historická. Praha, 1906. *Wilhelm,* II/*293 and 2519*.

PAUCKER, HENRI ROGER. Heinrich Heines dichterische Persoenlichkeit und deren Spiegelung in seinem Deutschland- und Frankreichbild. Bern, 1967. *Dissertation.*

PIERRE-GAUTHIEZ. Henri Heine. Paris (1913) *Wilhelm,* II/*115*.

PRÖHLE, HEINRICH. Heinrich Heine und der Harz. Harzburg, 1888. *Wilhelm,* II/*964*.

REINHARD, L. J. Heinrich Heine (Grosse Sowjet-Enzyklopädie) Berlin, 1954. *Seifert, 842.*

REMER, PAUL. Die freien Rhythmen in Heinrich
  Heines Nordseebildern. Heidelberg, 1889.
  Wilhelm, II/3092.

RUMPLER, SIEGFRIED NORBERT. Heinrich Heine.
  Ein Essay. Wien, 1907. *Wilhelm, II/298.*

SALTER, SIEGBERT (pseudonym of SIMON SALOMON)
  Heinrich Heine (Anekdoten aus dem Leben
  berühmter Männer. Band 1) Berlin (1906)
  Wilhelm, II/771.

SCHÖNFELDT, OTTO (editor) Und alle lieben Heinrich
  Heine . . . (Bürgerinitiative Heinrich-Heine-
  Universität Düsseldorf 1968–1972) Köln, 1972.

SEIFERT, SIEGFRIED (editor) Heine-Bibliographie
  1954–1964. Berlin and Weimar, 1968.

SPAETH, ALBERT. La Pensée de Henri Heine (Paris)
  1946. *Wilhelm, II/2036.*

STRÜMPELL, LUDWIG [Review of Heinrich Heine,
  Der Salon. Zweiter Band] Leipzig, 1895. *In:
  Abhandlungen aus dem Gebiet der Ethik . . .1.
  Heft. Wilhelm, II/3171.*

TONELLI, GIORGIO. Heine e la Germania (Palermo)
  1963. *Seifert, 1884.*

TREUMUND, CHRISTOPHORUS [pseudonym of
  FRIEDRICH SPIGL] Das Heinrich Heine-Denkmal
  oder: Der Scandal auf dem Parnasse. Ein
  dramatisches Capriccio. Wien, 1888. *Wilhelm,
  II/3986.*

VÉGA [pseudonym of MME. DE MISME] Henri Heine.
  Peint par lui-même et par les autres. Paris, 1936.
  Presentation copy. Wilhelm, II/139.

VERMEIL, EDMOND. Henri Heine, ses vues sur
  l'Allemagne et les révolutions européennes.
  Paris, 1939. *Wilhelm, II/2210.*

VICTOR, WALTHER. Mathilde. Ein Leben um
  Heinrich Heine. Leipzig and Wien, 1931.
  Wilhelm, II/1109.

WENDEL, HERMANN. Heinrich Heine. Ein Lebens-
  und Zeitbild. Berlin, 1926. *Wilhelm, II/117.*

Zeitschrift für Deutsche Philologie. 91. Band 1972.
  Sonderheft: Heine und seine Zeit. Berlin, 1972.

[*Heine, Salomon*] HEILBUT (DR.) Das neue
  Krankenhaus der Israelitischen Gemeinde in
  Hamburg, erbaut von Herrn Salomon Heine.
  Hamburg, 1843.

LUDWIG BOERNE

BÖRNE, LUDWIG. Berliner Briefe 1828 (editor, L.
  Geiger) Berlin, 1905.

BÖRNE, LUDWIG (editor) Die Wage. Eine Zeitschrift
  für Bürgerleben Wissenschaft und Kunst. Erster
  Band. Frankfurt am Main, 1818–1820. *Helmut

*Bock, Ludwig Boerne (Berlin, 1962), page 423, has
  "Waage" erroneously. Complete set consists of
  two volumes (thirteen numbers), 1818–1821.*

NOVÁK, ARNE. Menzel, Boerne, Heine. Studie
  literárně-historická. Praha, 1906. *Wilhelm, II/293,
  2519.*

ROTHSCHILDS

COWLES, VIRGINIA. The Rothschilds. A Family of
  Fortune. New York, 1973.

D***, A. Guerre aux Juifs! ou La Vérité sur MM. de
  Rothschild. Paris, 1846. *Eichstädt, 3000.*

GILLE, BERTRAND (editor) Lettres adressées à la
  maison Rothschild de Paris par son représentant à
  Bruxelles. II (L'époque des susceptibilités)
  1843–1853. Louvain and Paris, 1963.

[MATHIEU-DAIRNVAELL, GEORGES MARIE] Jugement
  rendu contre J. Rothschild et contre Georges
  Dairnvaell, Auteur de l'histoire de Rothschild Ier,
  par le Tribunal de la Saine Raison . . . Paris, 1846.
  Eichstädt, 2997.

PLAUT, RUDOLPH. Gedächtnis-Rede gehalten an der
  Bahre der verewigten Freifrau Carl von
  Rothschild . . . 1894. Frankfurt am Main (1894)

RAVAGE, M. E. Grandeur et Décadence de la Maison
  Rothschild. Paris (1931) *Presentation copy to
  John Gunther.*

Rothschild. Ein Urtheilsspruch vom menschlichen
  Standpunkte aus. Herisau, 1846. *Eichstädt, 2998.*

[*Rothschild, Edmund von*] HIRSCH, MENDEL.
  Worte bei der Vermählung des Freiherrn Edmund
  von Rothschild mit Freiin Adelheid von
  Rothschild . . . 1877 [Frankfurt am Main, 1877]

[*Rothschild, Hannah Louise von*] PLAUT, RUDOLPH.
  Gedächtnis-Rede, gehalten bei der Enthüllung des
  Grab-Denkmals der verewigten Freifräulein
  Hannah Louise von Rothschild . . .1893. Frankfurt
  am Main (1893)

Statut für die beiden dem Herrn Wilhelm Carl
  Freiherrn von Rothschild zu Frankfurt am Main
  zugehörigen grossen Gebäude auf dem
  sogenannten Deutsch-Israelitischen Platze in
  Jerusalem (Frankfurt am Main, 1881)

MARTIN BUBER

BUBER, MARTIN. Die Frage an den Einzelnen. Berlin,
  1936.

BUBER, MARTIN. Vom Geist des Judentums. Leipzig,
  1916.

Martin Buber. Reden und Aufsätze zum 80.
  Geburtstag. Düsseldorf, 1958.

HERMANN COHEN

COHEN, HERMANN. Innere Beziehungen der Kantischen Philosophie zum Judentum. Berlin, 1910. *In: 28. Bericht der Lehranstalt für die Wissenschaft des Judentums in Berlin.*

COHEN, HERMANN. Le Judaïsme et le Progrès Religieux de l'Humanité. Paris, 1911.

COHEN, HERMANN and ELBOGEN, I. Reden bei der Trauerfeier für Geheimen Justizrat Dr. Herman Veit Simon . . . 1915 in der Lehranstalt für die Wissenschaft des Judentums. Berlin, 1915 (1916?)

COHEN, HERMANN. Ausgewählte Stellen aus unveröffentlichten Briefen (Berlin) 1929.

KAPLAN, SIMON. Das Geschichtsproblem in der Philosophie Hermann Cohens. Berlin, 1930.

NATORP, PAUL. Hermann Cohen als Mensch, Lehrer und Forscher. Gedächtnisrede . . . 1918. Marburg, 1918.

ODEBRECHT, RUDOLF. Hermann Cohens Philosophie der Mathematik. Berlin, 1906. *Dissertation.*

UCKO, SIEGFRIED. Der Gottesbegriff in der Philosophie Hermann Cohens. Berlin, 1929.

ALBERT EINSTEIN

EINSTEIN, A. Näherungsweise Integration der Feldgleichungen der Gravitation. 1916. *Weil, 86; Schilpp, 99.*

EINSTEIN, ALBERT. Relativity. The Special and General Theory. New York, 1947.

Why War? The Correspondence between Albert Einstein and Sigmund Freud. Chicago, 1978.

BERNSTEIN, JEREMY. Albert Einstein. New York, 1972.

CUNY, HILAIRE. Albert Einstein. The Man and his Theories. Greenwich, 1965.

GAWRONSKY, D. Die Relativitätstheorie Einsteins im Lichte der Philosophie. Ein neuer Beweis der Lorentz-Transformationen. Bern, 1924.

MOREUX, TH. Pour comprendre Einstein . . . Paris, 1922.

REISER, ANTON [pseudonym of RUDOLF KAYSER] Albert Einstein. A Biographical Portrait. New York, 1930.

SEELIG, CARL (editor) Helle Zeit – Dunkle Zeit. In Memoriam Albert Einstein. Zürich, etc., 1956.

SIGMUND FREUD

Freudiana from the Collections of The Jewish National and University Library exhibited . . . 1973. Jerusalem, 1973.

Why War? The Correspondence between Albert Einstein and Sigmund Freud. Chicago, 1978.

LINK, CHRISTIAN. Theologische Perspektiven nach Marx und Freud. Stuttgart, etc., 1971.

SCHÖNAU, WALTER. Sigmund Freuds Prosa. Literarische Elemente seines Stils. Stuttgart, 1968. *Dissertation.*

MAXIMILIAN HARDEN

MEHRING, FRANZ. Herrn Hardens Fabeln. Berlin, 1899.

YOUNG, HARRY F. Maximilian Harden. Censor Germaniae. Ein Publizist im Widerstreit von 1892 bis 1927. Münster, 1971.

KARL KRAUS

KRAUS, KARL. Peter Altenberg (Rede am Grabe Peter Altenbergs 11. Januar 1919) Wien (1919)

KRAUS, KARL. Ausgewählte Gedichte. München, 1920.

KRAUS, KARL. Die demolirte Literatur. Steinbach, 1972.

KRAUS, KARL. Literatur und Lüge. Wien-Leipzig, 1929.

KRAUS, KARL. Nachts. Leipzig, 1918.

KRAUS, KARL. Sprüche und Widersprüche. Wien-Leipzig, 1924.

KRAUS, KARL. Wolkenkuckucksheim. Phantastisches Versspiel in drei Akten. Wien-Leipzig, 1923.

ENGELMANN, PAUL. Dem Andenken an Karl Kraus. Wien, 1967.

JÖRGENSEN, ALF. Karl Kraus. Der Heinefresser und die Ursachen. Eine Studie über moderne Journalistik. Flensburg [1912]

SCHEU, ROBERT. Karl Kraus. Wien, 1909.

WEIGEL, HANS. Karl Kraus oder die Macht der Ohnmacht. Wien, etc., 1968.

GUSTAV LANDAUER

LACHMANN, HEDWIG. Gesammelte Gedichte. Eigenes und Nachdichtungen (Herausgegeben von Gustav Landauer) Potsdam, 1919.

LINSE, ULRICH (editor) Gustav Landauer und die Revolutionszeit 1918/19. Berlin, 1974.

TAGORE, RABINDRANATH. Der König der dunklen Kammer (Übertragung von Hedwig Lachmann und Gustav Landauer) München [1919]

THEODOR LESSING

LESSING, THEODOR. Der fröhliche Eselsquell. Gedanken über Theater, Schauspieler, Drama. Berlin, 1912.

LESSING, THEODOR. Theater-Seele. Studie über Bühnenästhetik und Schauspielkunst. Berlin, 1907.

FRITZ MAUTHNER

MAUTHNER, FRITZ. Vom armen Franischko (Kleine Abenteuer eines Kesselflickers) Konstanz am Bodensee, 1917.

JOSEPH POPPER-LYNKEUS

POPPER-LYNKEUS, JOSEF. Mein Leben und Wirken. Eine Selbstdarstellung. Dresden, 1924.

FREI, BRUNO. Der Türmer [Josef Popper-Lynkeus] Wien, 1971.

SCHWARZ, RICHARD. Rathenau, Goldscheid, Popper-Lynkeus und ihre Systeme zusammengefasst zu einem Wirtschaftsprogramm. Wien-Leipzig, 1919.

WALTHER RATHENAU

RATHENAU, WALTHER. Impressionen. Leipzig, 1902. *With watermark in paper "W.R."*

RATHENAU, WALTHER. Tagebuch 1907–1922. Privatdruck. No place, 1930. *Numbered. Copy number 2.*

Walther Rathenau 1867–1922. Privatdruck. No place, 1932. *Numbered. Copy number 94.*

CAUER, PAUL. Walther Rathenaus staatsbürgerliches Programm. Berlin, 1918. *Gottlieb, E670.*

EBERHARDT, PAUL. Freundschaft im Geist. Briefwechsel mit Walther Rathenau. Nachgelassene Gedichte. Aufsätze. Gotha, 1927. *Gottlieb, E2220.*

SCHREIBER, GEORG. Walther Rathenau. I. Wissenschaftsplanung. II. Begegnung beim Reichsetat. No place, 1955. *Sonderdruck.*

SCHWARZ, RICHARD. Rathenau, Goldscheid, Popper-Lynkeus und ihre Systeme zusammengefasst zu einem Wirtschaftsprogramm. Wien-Leipzig, 1919. *Gottlieb, E854.*

SIMON, H. F. Aus Walther Rathenaus Leben. Dresden, 1927.

SOLZBACHER, WILHELM. Walther Rathenau als Sozialphilosoph. Die Überwindung der Entseelung. Köln, 1933.

FRANZ ROSENZWEIG

ROSENZWEIG, FRANZ. Jehuda Halevi. Zweiundneunzig Hymnen und Gedichte Deutsch. Berlin, no date.

ROSENZWEIG, FRANZ. Kleinere Schriften. Berlin, 1937.

ROSENSTOCK-HUESSY, EUGEN (editor) Judaism Despite Christianity. The "Letters on Christianity and Judaism" between Eugen Rosenstock-Huessy and Franz Rosenzweig. University, Alabama, 1969.

TEWES, JOSEPH. Zum Existenzbegriff Franz Rosenzweigs. Meisenheim am Glan, 1970.

ERNST TOLLER

TOLLER, ERNST. I was a German. An Autobiography. London, 1934.

JEWISH QUESTION IN GERMANY AND AUSTRIA

(*Ahlwardt*) JACOBOWSKI, LUDWIG. Offene Antwort eines Juden auf Herrn Ahlwardt's "Der Eid eines Juden." Berlin (1891)

[*Ahlwardt*] PLACK-PODGÒRSKI, RUDOLF. Ahlwardt vor Gericht. Eine kritische Beleuchtung des Judenflinten-Prozesses. Dresden, 1892.

[*Ahlwardt*] PLACK-PODGÒRSKI, RUDOLF. Pharisäer und Heuchler oder die Leuchten des deutschen Parlaments und die Stützen des Staates. Geschildert nach dem Ahlwardtschen Aktenmaterial . . . Berlin, no date.

Der neue Antisemitismus. Die Liquidierung von Ausländerorganisationen in der BRD: Zum Verbot von GUPS und GUPA. München, 1972.

ARMIN UND GOTTFRIED, BR[ÜDER] [pseudonym] Die Judenfrage. Mahnrufe an den deutschen V.A.O.D. Lorch [1920]

ARMIN, OTTO [pseudonym of ALFRED ROTH] Die Juden im Heere. Eine statistische Untersuchung nach amtlichen Quellen. München, 1919.

ARMIN, OTTO [pseudonym of ALFRED ROTH] Die Juden in den Kriegs-Gesellschaften und in der Kriegs-Wirtschaft. München, 1921.

ARMIN, OTTO [pseudonym of ALFRED ROTH] Von Rathenau zu Barmat. Der Leidensweg des deutschen Volkes. Stuttgart, 1925.

ARNOLD, FRIEDRICH (editor) Anschläge. Deutsche Plakate als Dokumente der Zeit 1900–1960. Ebenhausen bei München, 1963.

AUSTRIACUS [pseudonym] Wählet keinen Juden! Ein Mahn- und Warnungsruf an die Völker Oesterreich-Ungarns. Berlin, 1881.

BARTELS, ADOLF. Ein Berliner Litteraturhistoriker. Dr. Richard M. Meyer und seine "deutsche Litteratur." Leipzig and Berlin, 1900.

BEDA [pseudonym of DR. FRITZ LÖHNER] Getaufte und Baldgetaufte. Wien, etc., 1925.

[*Bleichröder*] CREMER, CHRISTOPH JOSEPH. Die angeblichen 10,000 Mark des Herrn von Bleichröder. Berlin, 1889.
See Stern, page 531, note.

[*Bleichröder*] Schwerin und Bleichröder. Edelmann und Jude. Dresden, 1893.

[*Bleichröder*] STERN, FRITZ. Gold and Iron. Bismarck, Bleichröder, and the Building of the German Empire. New York, 1977.

BLÜHER, HANS – page 273, right column, 3rd entry from bottom, is erroneous and to be deleted.

BRÜGGEN, ERNST VON DER. Das deutsche Judenthum in seiner Heimat (Leipzig, 1880) *In "Die Grenzboten."*

CASTNER, G. Die Kriegsschuldlüge im Lichte der jüdischen Weltherrschaft. Leipzig, 1927.

COHN, ALFRED. Die Juden und die Freimaurerei. Leipzig [1912]

"Daspejü." "Semi-Imperator." III. Teil. Sonderdruck: "Das spezifisch Jüdische." Leipzig, 1920.

Denkschrift über die Judenfrage in dem Gesetz betreffend den Austritt aus der Kirche. Berlin, 1873.

Deutsche und Juden ein unlösbares Problem. Reden zum Jüdischen Weltkongress 1966 [Düsseldorf] 1966.

Die Drohnen. Von einem Manne aus dem Volke. No place, no date.

Zu den Erlassen Sr. Majestät des Kaisers. Bemerkungen eines Juden. Berlin, 1891.

Sind die Freimaurer Judenknechte und Vaterlandsverderber? Hier ist die Antwort der Wahrheit! No place, no date.

GERBER, G. Warenhaus Pest. Dresden, no date.

GOLDSTEIN, JULIUS. Deutsche Volks-Idee und Deutsch-Völkische Idee. Berlin, 1927.

HALL-HALFEN, WILHELM. Der arisch-semitische Rassenwahn als Grundursache des Weltzusammenbruchs. Berlin [1920]

HEINRICH, A. Der Juden Einfluss. Eine religiöse, sittliche und wirtschaftliche Betrachtung. Winnenden, 1920.

HERMANN DER DEUTSCHE [pseudonym] . . . Die Verschwörung der Juden und Jesuiten gegen die Freiheit und Wohlfahrt des deutschen Volkes und gegen die Reichseinheit. Danzig, 1924.

HOFFMANN, ALBRECHT. Rom, Juda und wir. Lorch, 1924.

HUBERTUS, ROLAND. Warum verdient der Jude schneller und mehr Geld als der Christ? Berlin-Schöneberg, no date. *Zeitschrift zur Volksbelehrung Jahrg ang 1, Heft 1.*

J., J. Tante Eulalia und die Judenfrage. Die Einwände der Hebräerfreunde, widerlegt auf 9 Teeabenden. Am Schlusse: Wer ist die Tante Eulalia? Stettin, no date.

Wo Juden unerwünscht sind! Kurorte, Sommerfrischen usw. antisemitischen Charakters; Antisemitische Gaststätten und ausgesprochene "christliche" Häuser . . . No place, no date.

Unsere Judenfrage. Von einem Juden deutscher Kultur. Berlin, 1906.

Die Judenfrage vor dem Preussischen Landtage. Wortgetreuer Abdruck der Verhandlungen im Abgeordnetenhause . . . 1880. Berlin, 1880.

Was ist es mit der Judenfrage? Ein kurzes Wort zur Belehrung und Beherzigung. Neustettin, 1881.

JUNIUS [pseudonym of KARL FRANZ FROHME] Das Judenthum und die Tagespresse. Ein Mahnwort in ernster Stunde. Leipzig, 1879.

JUNIUS [pseudonym of KARL FRANZ FROHME] Paul Lindau und das literarische Judenthum. Eine Controverspredigt aus der Gegenwart. Leipzig, no date. *Third edition.*

JUNIUS [pseudonym of KARL FRANZ FROHME] "Philister über Dir!" Berlin, 1890.

KAHN, SIEGBERT. Antisemitismus und Rassenhetze. Eine Übersicht über ihre Entwicklung in Deutschland. Berlin, 1948.

Der Jüdische Kriegsplan zur Aufrichtung der Judenweltherrschaft im Jahre des Heils 1925. Nach den Richtlinien der Weisen von Zion. Lorch (Württemberg) [1925]

KUNZE, RICHARD (editor) Im neuen Deutschland! Ein Bilderbuch für Erwachsene. Berlin-Friedenau, 1921.

LEHMANN, J. A. EMIL. Der Deutsche jüdischen Bekenntnisses. Vortrag . . . Berlin, 1894.

LERIQUE, JOSEPH. Das Judenthum in der deutschen Literatur. Frankfurt am Main, 1882.

LIEK, WALTER [pseudonym of HANS VON LIEBIG] Der Anteil des Judentums am Zusammenbruche Deutschlands. München, 1921.

LIEK, WALTER (pseudonym of HANS VON LIEBIG] Der deutsche Arbeiter und das Judentum. München, 1924.

[*Lueger*] KUPPE, RUDOLF. Dr. Karl Lueger. Persönlichkeit und Wirken. Wien, 1947.

[*Lueger*] SCHNEE, HEINRICH. Bürgermeister Karl Lueger. Leben und Wirken eines grossen Deutschen. Paderborn, 1936.

[*Lueger*] STAURACZ, FRANZ. Dr. Karl Lueger. Zehn Jahre Bürgermeister. Wien and Leipzig, 1907.

LÜTTWITZ, ARTHUR MARIA BARON VON. Wir sind die Juden. Eine biblische Studie. Berlin [1894]

LYNKEUS [pseudonym] Der deutsche Buchhandel und das Judentum. Ein Menetekel. Leipzig, 1925.

MAIER, GUSTAV. Mehr Licht! Ein Wort zur "Judenfrage" an unsere christlichen Mitbürger. Ulm, 1881.

MARR, WILHELM. Judarnas seger över Germanerna. En social-politisk och kulturhistorisk Studie. Helsingfors, 1921.

MOHRMANN, WALTER. Antisemitismus. Ideologie und Geschichte im Kaiserreich und in der Weimarer Republik. Berlin, 1972.

NAUDH, H. [pseudonym of H. NORDMANN] Minister Maybach und Der "Giftbaum." Berlin, 1880.

OPPELN-BRONIKOWSKI, FRIEDRICH VON. Antisemitismus? Eine unparteiische Prüfung des Problems. Charlottenburg, 1920.

OPPLER, FRIEDRICH. Das falsche Tabu. Betrachtungen über das deutsch-jüdische Problem. Stuttgart, 1966.

OREL, ANTON. Judaismus oder deutsche Romantik? Wien, 1921.

PAASCH, CARL. Mein gutes Recht. Zürich, 1906.

[PERROT, FRANZ FÜRCHTEGOTT] Die Aera Bleichröder-Delbrück-Camphausen. Berlin, 1876.

PLATH, KARL HEINRICH CHRISTIAN. Was machen wir Christen mit unsern Juden!? Nördlingen, 1881.

PREISSLER, HEINRICH. Die Schandpresse von Neu-Jerusalem (Wien, 1872)

PREISSLER, HEINRICH. Das Trottelthum in Neu-Jerusalem (Wien, 1872)

R., B. Die Magdeburger "Israelitische Wochenschrift" und ihr Rath an die Juden bezüglich der Militair-Vorlage. Magdeburg, 1893.

RAM, RENATUS. Godentum und Judaismus. Wegweiser in die Deutsche Zukunft. Rudolstadt, 1921.

REBBERT, JOSEPH. Blicke in's Talmudische Judenthum. Nach den Forschungen von Dr. Konrad Martin, Bischof von Paderborn, dem christlichen Volke enthüllt. Paderborn, 1876.

RECKE (GRAF) Judentum und Freimaurerei. Kolberg (1917) *Wiener, 5/1073.*

REICHMANN, EVA G. Flucht in den Hass. Die Ursachen der deutschen Judenkatastrophe. Frankfurt am Main, 1968.

REUMANN, JAKOB. Nieder mit den Schurken die dem Volk das Fleisch vertheuern oder Wiener Fleischwucher und antisemitischer Gemeinderath. Wien, no date.

RICHTER, HANS. Judenhetze! Aussig, 1924.

ROTH, ALFRED. Der Judenpranger. Ein Spiegelbild der jüdischen Seele dargestellt an namenlosen Briefen und Zuschriften von Juden und Jüdinnen gerichtet an A. R. Hamburg, 1922.

S., F. Der Antisemitismus der Gegenwart und seine Abwehr. Ein Weckruf an die deutschen Juden. Mülheim am Rhein, 1895.

SCHÖLER, H. Die Antisemiten, ihre Programme und ihre Leute. Vortrag . . . Dresden, 1894.

SCHÖNBACH, PETER. Reaktionen auf die antisemitische Welle im Winter 1959/1960. Frankfurt am Main, 1961.

SCHÖNERER, GEORG. Rede . . . gehalten in der . . . 1904 zu Eger stattgehabten alldeutschen Versammlung (Schloss Rosenau bei Zwettl, 1904)

SCHÖNERER, GEORG RITTER VON. Reden. Horn, 1896.

SCHÖNERER, GEORG. Zur Sprachenfrage. Rede. Horn, 1898.

[*Schönerer*] Georg R. von Schönerer. Zu seinem Tode. Wien, 1930.

[*Schönerer*] HERWIG [pseudonym of] EDUARD PICHL. Georg Schönerer und die Entwicklung des Alldeutschtumes in der Ostmark. 4 volumes. Wien, 1912, 1913, 1914, 1923 [Also] PICHL, EDUARD. Georg Schönerer, Volumes 5 and 6 in 1 volume. Oldenburg, 1938.

SCHORSCH, ISMAR. Jewish Reactions to German Anti-Semitism, 1870–1914. New York, etc., 1972.

SCHRATTENHOLZ, JOSEF. Vor dem Scheiterhaufen. Ein Wort für die Juden und ein Vorwort für den Czaaren. Breslau, 1891.

Jüdische Selbstbekenntnisse. Leipzig, 1919.

Jüdische Sitten-Gesetze (Auszug aus dem Talmud und Schulchan Aruch) Lorch (Württemberg) 1922.

ST., J. Vier Sendschreiben an die Hebräer deutscher Zunge oder: Briefliche Correspondenz zwischen einem katholischen Pfarrer und einem Rabbiner. München, 1871. *On cover: Augsburg.*

TEJA, HEINZ. Die Maske herunter! Ein Beitrag zur Judenfrage in Deutschland. Berlin, 1904.

TRÜTZSCHLER, FRITZ VON. Armes Volkstum! oder Der deutsche Bürger am Juden gemessen! Eine Streitschrift wider und für die Deutschen! von einem Lehndeutschen. Berlin-Wilmersdorf, 1920.

Umsturz ihr Stern! Bleiben sie Herr'n? Bayr. Mittelpartei (Deutschnationale Volkspartei in Bayern) München (about 1920) *Broadside.*

Die Vernichtung des Deutschen Reiches und Volkes jetzt unmittelbar bevorstehend! Lorch-Württemberg (1932)

WAHRMUND [pseudonym] Los vom Antisemitismus! Offener Brief an einen Unverfälschten. Linz, 1891.

WALDEGG, EGON [pseudonym of ALEXANDER PINKERT] Judenhetze oder Nothwehr? Ein Mahnwort. Dresden, 1880.

WEISS, CHRISTOPH. Vom Juden-Sozialismus geheilt! Meinen deutschen Arbeitsbrüdern und Arbeitsschwestern zur Aufklärung. Lorch, 1920.

WELCKER, VIKTOR HUGO. Die nationalen und sozialen Aufgaben des Antisemitismus. Ulm, 1882.

Der Weltkampf. Monatsschrift für die Judenfrage aller Länder. 1. Jahrgang, Heft 2. München, 1924.

Der Weltkampf. Monatsschrift für Weltpolitik, völkische Kultur und die Judenfrage aller Länder. Heft 24, 29, 37, 48, 63, 66. München, 1925, 1926, 1927, 1929.

MARTIN LUTHER

LUTHER, MARTINUS. Das Jhesus Christus ain geborner Jude sey. Wittemberg, 1523. *Benzing, 1535. Printed by M. Ramminger, Augsburg. The edition in Cat., page 289, is Benzing, 1531, printed by Melchior Lotter d. J., Wittenberg.*

STEINLEIN, H. Luthers Stellung zum Judentum. Nürnberg, 1929.

VOGELSANG, ERICH. Luthers Kampf gegen die Juden. Tübingen, 1933.

HOUSTON STEWART CHAMBERLAIN

CHAMBERLAIN, HOUSTON STEWART. Arische Weltanschauung. München, 1934. *Seventh edition.*

CHAMBERLAIN, HOUSTON STEWART. Der Wille zum Sieg und andere Aufsätze. München, 1918.

BEYER, HERMANN WOLFGANG. Houston Stewart Chamberlain und die innere Erneuerung des Christentums. Berlin, 1939.

FOERSTER, FR. W. England in H. St. Chamberlains Beleuchtung. Ein Protest. München, 1917.

SEILLIÈRE, ERNEST. Houston-Stewart Chamberlain. Le plus récent philosophe du pangermanisme mystique. Paris, 1917.

VOLLRATH, WILHELM. Th. Carlyle und H. St. Chamberlain, zwei Freunde Deutschlands. München, 1935.

ADOLF STOECKER

STÖCKER, ADOLF. Stöcker in Freiberg. "Das deutsche Volk im Kampfe mit seinen Verderbern." Vortrag … gehalten … 1891 (Freiberg) 1891.

BRAUN, MAX. Adolf Stoecker. Berlin (1913)

KRAUSE, VON (OBERST Z.D., editor) Zum Austritt Stöckers aus der konservativen Partei. Berlin, 1896.

MEHRING, FRANZ. Herr Hofprediger Stöcker der Socialpolitiker. Eine Streitschrift. Bremen, 1882.

[UNGERN-STERNBERG, ALEXANDER FREIHERR VON] Der falsche und der wahre Stöcker. Von einem Mitgliede des Deutschen Reichstags. Leipzig, 1885.

WITTE, CARL. Schneider Grüneberg und Hofprediger Stöcker oder Der gefälschte Brief. Berlin, 1896.

AUGUST ROHLING

ROHLING, AUG. (editor) Das Buch des Propheten Daniel. Mainz, 1876.

ROHLING, AUG. Talmud-Jude. Mit einem Vorworte von Eduard Drumont aus der … französischen Ausgabe von A. Pontigny in das Deutsche zurückübertragen von Carl Paasch. Leipzig, no date. *Seventh edition.*

ROHLING, AUG. Talmudský Žid. Přerovê, no date.

ROSENBACHER, ARNOLD. Vortrag … über das Kopp'sche Werk (Stritt Rohling-Bloch) Prag, 1886.

PALESTINE

ACCOLTUS, BENEDICTUS. De bello a Christianis contra barbaros gesto, pro Christi sepulcro, & Iudea recuperandis. Libri IIII. Florentiae, 1623.

AMMANN, HANS JAKOB. Reiss Ins Globte Land … Zürich, 1919. *Reprint of: Zurich, 1630.*

BARAMKI, DIMITRI C. The Art and Architecture of Ancient Palestine. Beirut, Lebanon, 1969.

BOCK, EMIL. Palästina. Tagebücher von zwei Reisen. Stuttgart, 1935.

LEVINSOHN, ISSAC. The Story of My Wanderings in "The Land of My Fathers." London and Glasgow, 1903.

MALLMIN, JOHANNES ERICUS. Dissertatio de jure Israëlitarum Palaestinam occupandi. Upsaliae, 1788.

NOE [BIANCHI] (editor) Viaggio da Venetia al S. Sepalcro, et al Monte Sinai … Bassano, no date. *Tobler, page 64: 1675 or 1685; Graesse, I, 361: 1680.*

PROKESCH RITTER VON OSTEN, A. Reise ins heilige Land. Im Jahr 1829. Wien, 1831.

ROBERTUS [ROBERT LEOB] Der Andächtige Pilgrim, oder . . . Beschreibung der Reise, welche . . . Herr Robertus . . . In das heilige Land und nach Jerusalem glücklich hinterleget. Nürnberg, 1740. *Tobler, page 123.*

ROTH, ERWIN. Preussens Gloria im Heiligen Land. Die Deutschen und Jerusalem. München (1973)

SCHNELLER, LUDWIG. Die Kaiserfahrt durchs Heilige Land. Leipzig, 1899.

SCHNELLER, LUDWIG. Vater Schneller. Ein Patriarch der Evangelischen Mission im Heiligen Lande. Leipzig, 1925.

TIBAWI, A. L. Jerusalem. Its Place in Islam and Arab History. Beirut, 1969.

TUCHER, HANNS [Reise in das gelobte Land] Nürnberg [K. Zeninger] 1483. *Hain, 15666.*

ZIONISM AND JEWISH NATIONALISM

BERGER, ELMER. Emancipation: the Rediscovered Ideal. Philadelphia (1945)

BLUMENFELD, KURT. Im Kampf um den Zionismus. Briefe aus fünf Jahrzehnten. Stuttgart, 1976.

BÖHM, ADOLF. Die zionistische Bewegung 1918 bis 1925. Berlin, 1937.

BÖHM, ADOLF. Der Jüdische Nationalfonds, ein Instrument zur Abhilfe der Judennot. Köln and Leipzig, 1910.

BOLSHAKOV, V. Anti-Communism, the Main Line of Zionism. Moscow, 1972.

DERAW, ALEXANDER. Palästina das Heilige Land ein souveräner jüdischer Staat? Berlin, 1919.

CALVARY, M. Die Aufgabe des deutschen Zionismus. Berlin-Charlottenburg, no date. *Offprint.*

GOLDMANN, NACHUM. Our Position in the World of Today and Tomorrow. New York, 1945.

HABER, JULIUS. The Odyssey of an American Zionist. Fifty Years of Zionist History. New York, 1956.

HARDAN, DAVID (editor) Sources. Anthology of Contemporary Jewish Thought. Number 1. Jerusalem, 1970.

HOLDHEIM, GERHARD. Der politische Zionismus. Werden, Wescn, Entwicklung. Alfeld, 1964.

HOLDHEIM, GERHARD AND PREUSS, WALTER. Die theoretischen Grundlagen des Zionismus. Berlin, 1919.

IVANOV, YURI. Caution: Zionism! Essays on the Ideology, Organisation and Practice of Zionism. Moscow, 1970.

Unsere Judenfrage. Von einem Juden deutscher Kultur. Berlin, 1906. *Freimann, page 327.*

LEWISOHN, LUDWIG. Israel. New York, 1925. *Presentation copy inscribed by Ludwig Lewisohn to Dr. Chaim Weizmann.*

LIPSKY, LOUIS. Zionism and Arab Fears. New York, 1937.

LUMER, HYMAN. Zionism. Its Role in World Politics. New York, 1973.

MAGIL, JOSEPH (editor) Collection of Zionistic and National Songs . . . Philadelphia, Pennsylvania, 1903.

MEHEMED EMIN EFENDI (pseudonym of DR. S. LICHTENSTAEDTER) Die Zukunft Palästinas. Ein Mahnruf an die zionistischen Juden und an die ganze Kulturwelt. Frankfurt am Main, 1918.

MENUHIN, MOSHE. Quo Vadis Zionist Israel? A 1969 Postscript to The Decadence of Judaism in Our Time. Beirut, 1969.

MILLER, S. A. Internationalism and Zionism. London, 1936.

The Jewish People and Palestine. A Bibliophilic Pilgrimage Through Five Centuries. Cambridge, Massachusetts, 1973. *Exhibition catalogue at Harvard.*

PRAHYE, B. Deceived by Zionism. Moscow, 1971.

"Pro en Contra." Zionisme. Pro: Mr. S. Franzie Berenstein. Contra: A. B. Davids. Baarn, 1908.

ROTHSCHILD, ELI. Die Juden und das Heilige Land. Zur Geschichte des Heimkehrwillens eines Volkes. Hannover, 1971.

ROTHSCHILD, ELI (editor) Meilensteine. Vom Wege des Kartells Jüdischer Verbindungen (K. J. V.) in der zionistischen Bewegung . . . Tel-Aviv, 1972.

RUBIN, ELI (SOZIUS) Illusion Judenstaat Palästina. Wien, 1937.

SACHER, H. (editor) Het Zionisme en de toekomst der Joden. Deel I. Deventer, no date. *All published?*

SACHSE, HEINRICH (pseudonym of HEINRICH LÖWE) Antisemitismus und Zionismus. Eine zeitgemässe Betrachtung. Berlin, no date.

SCHWAB, HERMANN. Orthodoxie und Zionismus. Ein Wort zu den Geisteskämpfen der Gegenwart. Zürich [1919]

SCIAKY, ISACCO. Il Sionismo. Firenze, 1929. *Offprint.*

SEIDEN, RUDOLF. Um Zion und Zionismus. Hannover, 1925.

STRICKER, ROBERT. Die Vertreter des jüdischen Volkes. Wien, 1919.

TSCHLENOW, E. W. Der Krieg, die russische
Revolution und der Zionismus. Rede . . .
Copenhagen, 1917.

Die Wahrheit über Charkow. Herausgegeben von
der freien zionistischen Gruppe "Erez Israel" zu
Berlin . . . 1904. Berlin-Charlottenburg (1904)

WELTSCH, ROBERT. An der Wende des modernen
Judentums. Betrachtungen aus fünf Jahrzehnten.
Tübingen, 1972.

Who is Left? Zionism Answers Back. Jerusalem, 1971.

MODERN PALESTINE AND JEWISH COLONIZATION

ALGENSTAEDT, LUISE. Ums Land der Väter. Berlin-
Lichterfelde, 1912.

Alijah. Informationen für Palästina Auswanderer.
Berlin, 1935.

ARNHOLD, ERNA. Was ich in Palästina sah.
Breslau, 1927.

Britain's Problem in Palestine. The present position
in Palestine as reflected in the English Press.
Jerusalem, 1936.

CHURCHILL, WINSTON. Britische Politik in Palästina
Berlin, 1922.

CROSSMANN, R. H. S. AND FOOT, MICHAEL.
A Palestine Munich? London, 1946.

Documents Relating to the Balfour Declaration and
the Palestine Mandate. London, 1939.

FRIEDMAN, ISAIAH. German Intervention on Behalf
of the Yishuv, 1917. New York, 1971. *Offprint.*

FRUMKIN, H. Krise in Palästina? Tatsachen und
Perspektiven der Palästinawirtschaft auf Grund
der Ergebnisse von 1932 bis 1935. Berlin, 1936.

GRÜNBAUM, JOSEF. Das Land das Jedem heilig ist.
Miscellen aus einer palästinensischen
Reisegesellschaft. Budapest, 1912.

Habinjan. Sammelschrift des Habonim. Berlin, 1936.

Haboneh. Berlin, 1933.

Haboneh. Sammelschrift des Habonim anlässlich
seines fünfjährigen Bestehens. Berlin, 1938.

HERRMANN, HUGO. Eine werdende Welt.
Reiseeindrücke aus Palästina. Prag, 1925.

The Jewish National Home in Palestine. Hearings
before the Committee on Foreign Affairs House of
Representatives Seventy-Eighth Congress Second
Session . . . (editor, Ben Halpern) New York, 1970.

KAPLANSKY, SOLOMON. Probleme der Palästina-
Kolonisation. Berlin, 1923.

MANNHEIMER, GEORG. Palästina. Drei Akte aus dem
Leben der jüdischen Kolonisten. Prag, 1928.

NOACK, FRITZ. Briuth. Gesundheitsratgeber für
Palästina. Berlin, 1936.

Palästina und der Neubeginn jüdischen Lebens. Eine
Umschau in den Schriften des Keren Hajessod
(Berlin) no date.

RADLER-FELDMANN, J. Zur Arabischen Frage. Ein
Wort in zwölfter Stunde! Jerusalem (1936)

SACHSE, HEINRICH (pseudonym of HEINRICH LÖWE)
Zionistenkongress und Zionismus . . . eine Gefahr?
Berlin, 1897.

Das Schulwerk der Palästina-Commission der
"Freien Vereinigung" im heiligen Lande.
Frankfurt am Main (1914)

SUSSNITZKI, ALPHONS. Das jüdische Problem in
Palästina. Berlin, 1921.

[*Trumpeldor*] PROPES, ARON. Das Leben Josef
Trumpeldors. Vorwort von Vladimir Jabotinsky.
Riga, 1928.

STATE OF ISRAEL

The ABC of the Palestine Problem. Part 1,
1896–1949, Published by: The Arab Women's
Information Committee. Beirut, Lebanon, no date.

ABDEL-WAHAB M. EL-MESSIRI. Israel: Base of
Western Imperialism. New York, 1970.

Aims of the Palestinian Resistance Movement with
Regard to the Jews. Quotations from Resistance
leaders and documents. Beirut, Lebanon [1970]

AL-ABID, IBRAHIM (editor) Selected Essays on the
Palestine Question. Beirut, Lebanon, 1969.

AL-ABID, IBRAHIM. A Handbook to the Palestine
Question. Questions & Answers. Beirut,
Lebanon, 1969.

AL-ABID, IBRAHIM. Israel and Human Rights.
Beirut, Lebanon, 1969.

American Academic Association for Peace in the
Middle East. Proceedings of the Annual
Conference: The Anatomy of Peace in the Middle
East. New York, 1969.

APTHEKER, HERBERT. The Mid-East – Which Way to
Peace? New York, 1971.

The Arabs under Israeli Occupation. Memorandum
by The Arab Women's Information Committee . . .
Beirut, 1968.

The Arab-Israeli Armistice Agreements
February–July 1949. U.N. Texts and Annexes.
Beirut, Lebanon, 1967.

Two Articles on Palestine from the New Left Review. Washington, District of Columbia [1971]

AVNERY, URI. Israel ohne Zionisten. Plädoyer für eine neue Staatsidee. Gütersloh, 1969.

BUCH, PETER. Burning Issues of the Mideast Crisis. New York [1970]

(BUCH, PETER) Zionism and the Arab Revolution. The Myth of Progressive Israel. New York, 1969.

(CHALIAND, GERARD) The Palestinian Resistance Movement (in early 1969) Beirut, Lebanon (1969)

CHALIAND, GÉRARD. The Palestinian Resistance. Harmondsworth, 1972.

(CHILDERS, ERSKINE) The Other Exodus. No place, no date.

Christians, Zionism and Palestine. Beirut, Lebanon, 1970.

CORBON, JEAN. Western Public Opinion and the Palestine Conflict. Beirut, Lebanon (1969)

The Deceived Testify. Concerning the Plight of Immigrants in Israel. Moscow, 1971. *First edition: 36 pages.*

The Deceived Testify. Concerning the Plight of Immigrants in Israel. Moscow, 1972. *Second edition: 64 pages.*

DIB, GEORGE AND JABBER, FUAD. Israel's Violation of Human Rights in the Occupied Territories. A Documented Report (Beirut) 1970.

DOBBING, HERBERT. Cause for Concern. A Quaker's view of the Palestine Problem. Beirut, 1970.

Documents of the Palestinian Resistance Movement. New York, 1971.

DODD, PETER AND BARAKAT, HALIM. River without Bridges. A Study of The Exodus of the 1967 Palestinian Arab Refugees. Beirut, 1969.

Education in Israel. Report of the Select Subcommittee on Education. Committee on Education and Labor, House of Representatives; Ninety-First Congress, Second Session. Washington, 1970.

EL KODSY, AHMAD AND LOBEL, ELI. The Arab World and Israel. New York and London, 1970.

FRANKEL, DAVE VERSUS TOM FOLEY. Self-Determination in the Mideast. New York, 1974.

FREI, BRUNO (pseudonym of BENEDIKT FREISTADT) Israel zwischen den Fronten. Utopie und Wirklichkeit. Wien, etc., 1965.

GEORGE, MANFRED. Das Wunder Israel. Eindrücke von einer Reise durch den jungen jüdischen Staat. New York, 1950.

GERIES, SABRI AND LOBEL, ELI. Die Araber in Israel München, 1970.

HADAWI, SAMI. The Arab-Israeli Conflict (Cause and Effect) Beirut, 1969.

HADAWI, SAMI. Palestine in Focus. Beirut, Lebanon, 1969.

HERMAN, SIMON N. Israelis and Jews. The Continuity of an Identity. Philadelphia, 1971.

HOCHMAN, LARRY. Zionism and the Israeli State. Boston, Massachusetts, no date.

Israel and the Arabs. Militant Readers Debate the Mideast Conflict. New York [1969]

JABBER, FUAD A. (editor) International Documents on Palestine 1967. Beirut, 1970.

JANSEN, G. H. Zionism, Israel and Asian Nationalism. Beirut, 1971.

JANSEN, MICHAEL E. The United States and the Palestinian People. Beirut, 1970.

JIRYIS, SABRI. The Arabs in Israel. Beirut, Lebanon, 1969.

JIRYIS, SABRI. The Arabs in Israel (A Digest) Beirut, Lebanon (1969)

KADI, LEILA S. Basic Political Documents of the Armed Palestinian Resistance Movement. Beirut, Lebanon, 1969.

LANDMANN, MICHAEL. Das Israelpseudos der Pseudolinken. Antwort an Isaak Deutscher [and two other contributions] Berlin, 1971.

LUMER, HYMAN. Israel Today: War or Peace? New York, 1970.

MAJDALANY, JIBRAN. On the Necessity for an Anti-Racialist Solution to the Palestine Conflict. Beirut, Lebanon (1969)

MAZZAWI, MUSA. The Arab Refugees. A Tragic and Political Problem (London, 1968)

MERCHAV, PERETZ. Die israelische Linke. Zionismus und Arbeiterbewegung in der Geschichte Israels. Frankfurt am Main, 1972.

MEYSELS, THEODOR F. Israel in your pocket. 3 volumes. Jerusalem, 1955.

Middle East: Way to a Just Peace. Questions and Answers. Moscow, 1970.

NIKITINA, GALINA. The State of Israel. A Historical, Economic and Political Study. Moscow, 1973.

The Palestine Problem. Israel and Imperialism. Boston, Massachusetts (1968) *By members of Israeli Socialist Organization.*

PETRAN, TABITHA. Zionism. A Political Critique. Boston, Massachusetts, no date.

Die Prozesse von Haifa. Dokumente des gemeinsamen Widerstandes von Juden und Arabern – Früjahr 1973. Westberlin, 1973.

RASHEED, MOHAMMAD. Towards a Democratic State in Palestine. Beirut, Lebanon, 1970.

The Resistance of the Western Bank of Jordan to Israeli Occupation 1967. Beirut, Lebanon, 1967.

Return to 1947? (Israel Ministry of Foreign Affairs) Jerusalem, no date.

The Rights and Claims of Moslems and Jews in Connection with the Wailing Wall at Jerusalem. Beirut, 1968.

RODINSON, MAXIME. Israel and the Arabs. Baltimore, Maryland, 1969.

SAYEGH, ANIS. Palestine and Arab Nationalism. Beirut, Lebanon, 1970.

SAYEGH, FAYEZ A. Zionist Colonialism in Palestine. Beirut, Lebanon, 1965.

SAYEGH, FAYEZ A. The Zionist Diplomacy. Beirut, Lebanon, 1969.

SAYEGH, FAYEZ A. A Palestinian View. No place, no date.

SAYIGH, YUSIF A. Towards Peace in Palestine. Beirut, Lebanon (1970)

Seminar of Arab Jurists on Palestine. Algiers . . . 1967. The Palestine Question. Beirut, 1968.

SHARABI, HISHAM. Palestine Guerrillas. Their Credibility and Effectiveness. Beirut, Lebanon, 1970.

SHARIF, AMER A. A Statistical Study on the Arab Boycott of Israel. Beirut, Lebanon, 1970.

SHIBL, YUSUF (editor) Essays on the Israeli Economy. Beirut, Lebanon (1968)

SIRHAN, BASSEM. Palestinian Children: "The Generation of Liberation." Beirut, Lebanon, 1970.

STONE, I. F. For a New Approach to the Israeli-Arab Conflict (New York, 1967)

A Strategy for the Liberation of Palestine. Amman, 1969. *Published by The Popular Front for the Liberation of Palestine (P.F.L.P.)*

Political and Armed Struggle. No place, no date. *Published by The Palestine National Liberation Movement Fateh.*

TAYLOR, ALAN R. Prelude to Israel. An Analysis of Zionist Diplomacy 1897–1947. Beirut, Lebanon, 1970.

TOUMA, EMILE. About the idea of a Palestinian State. New York, 1970.

Towards a Democratic Solution to the Palestinian Question. Montreal, no date. *Published by The Democratic Peoples' Front for the Liberation of Palestine (DPFLP)*

WEINSTOCK, NATHAN AND ROTHSCHILD, JON. The Truth about Israel and Zionism. New York, 1970.

WINSTON, HENRY. Black Americans and the Middle East Conflict. New York, 1970.

ZAHLAN, ANTOINE. Science and Higher Education in Israel. Beirut, Lebanon, 1970.

ANTI-ISRAEL

ABU-GHAZALEH, ADNAN MOHAMMED. Arab Cultural Nationalism in Palestine during the British Mandate. Beirut and Benghazi, 1973.

ASHKAR, RIAD AND KHALIDI, AHMED. Weapons and Equipment of the Israeli Armed Forces. Beirut, 1971.

BERGER, ELMER. Letters and Non-Letters. The White House, Zionism and Israel. Beirut, 1972.

EL-ABID, IBRAHIM. Gewalt und Frieden. Eine Studie über die zionistische Strategie. Rastatt, 1969.

HADAWI, SAMI. Bittere Ernte. Palästina 1914–1967. Rastatt, 1969.

Internationales Israel-Hearing. Für Frieden und Gerechtigkeit im Nahen Osten. Protokoll Bonn, 15. Juni 1973. No place, no date [1973]

JIRYIS, SABRI. Democratic Freedoms in Israel. Beirut and Benghazi, 1972.

KHALED, LEILA. Mein Volk soll leben. Autobiographie der palästinensischen Revolutionärin. München, 1974.

KHALIDI, WALID. Das Palästinaproblem. Ursachen und Entwicklung 1897–1948. Rastatt, 1972.

MAROUN, SALAH. Der Westen und Palästina. Rastatt, 1973.

SAYEGH, FAYEZ A. Der zionistische Kolonialismus in Palästina. Die Vereinten Nationen und die Palästinafrage. Rastatt, 1968.

ZIONIST CONGRESSES

Festcommers zu Ehren des IX. Zionisten-Kongresses zu Hamburg am 28. Dez. 1909 (Hamburg, 1909)

Präsenz-Liste des Zionisten-Kongresses 1897–5657. Basel . . . Basel, 1897. *See Herzl Year Book, Volume 6, page 134.*

NORDAU, MAX. Vierter Zionisten-Kongress. Bericht über den Zustand der Juden auf der ganzen Welt. No place [1900?]

KOLLENSCHER, MAX. Binjan Haarez. Ein Wort an den XII. Zionisten-Kongress. Berlin, 1921.

Report of the Rescue Committee of the Jewish Agency for Palestine. Submitted to the Twenty-Second Zionist Congress at Basle . . . 1946. Jerusalem, 1946.

ZIONIST ORGANIZATION, JEWISH AGENCY, ETC. PUBLICATIONS

Memorandum des Bundesvorstands des Niederländischen Zionistenbundes an die Executive der Zionistischen Organisation. (Rotterdam) 1932.

MALLISON, W. T. The Legal Problems Concerning the Juridical Status and Political Activities of the Zionist Organization/Jewish Agency: A Study in International and U.S. Law. Beirut, 1968.

[*Jewish Agency*] The Palestine Issue. A Factual Analysis. Submitted to the Members of the United Nations by the Jewish Agency for Palestine 1947 [New York] 1947.

Executive of the World Zionist Organization and the Jewish Agency. Report on activities . . . 1962 submitted to the Session of the Zionist General Council Jerusalem, March 1963. Jerusalem, 1963.

ZIONISTISCHE VEREINIGUNG FÜR DEUTSCHLAND, BERLIN. Beiträge zur Frage unserer Propaganda. Ein Briefwechsel zwischen Herrn R. A. Max Jacobsohn und Herrn Kurt Blumenfeld, nebst Aeusserungen führender deutscher Zionisten. Berlin, 1928.

LEAGUE OF NATIONS AND UNITED NATIONS PUBLICATIONS

Annexes, Appendices and Maps to the Report by the United Nations Special Committee on Palestine to the General Assembly, Geneva, Switzerland . . . 1947. London, 1947.

PALESTINE GOVERNMENT PUBLICATIONS

Palästina-Bericht der britisch-amerikanischen Untersuchungskommission. Wien, 1946.

Parliamentary Debates (Hansard) House of Commons Official Report. Volume 445, Number 38. 11th December, 1947. London [1948] *Columns 1213–1525: Debate on the Partition of Palestine.*

BALFOUR DECLARATION

JEFFRIES, J. M. N. The Balfour Declaration. Beirut, Lebanon, 1969.

NEHER-BERNHEIM, RENÉE. La Déclaration Balfour. (Paris) 1969.

HISTORY OF ZIONISM

AUERBACH, ELIAS. Pionier der Verwirklichung. Ein Arzt aus Deutschland erzählt vom Beginn der zionistischen Bewegung und seiner Niederlassung in Palästina kurz nach der Jahrhundertwende. Stuttgart, 1969.

LAQUEUR, WALTER. A History of Zionism. New York, etc., 1972.

LICHTHEIM, RICHARD. Rückkehr. Lebenserinnerungen aus der Frühzeit des deutschen Zionismus. Stuttgart, 1970.

POLLAK, ADOLF. Zionismus. Eine historische Darstellung . . . nebst einer Chronik. Berlin, 1934.

ROSENBLATT, BERNARD A. Two Generations of Zionism. Historical Recollections of an American Zionist. New York, 1967.

ROTHSCHILD, ELI (editor) Meilensteine. Vom Wege des Kartells Jüdischer Verbindungen (K.J.V.) in der Zionistischen Bewegung. Tel Aviv, 1972.

SILBERBUSCH, JULIAN. Einführung in den Zionismus. III: Geschichte des Zionismus. Praha, 1936.

ZINEMAN, JACOB. Histoire du Sionisme. Paris, 1950.

ZIONISM, *Forerunners*

BICKERSTETH, E. The Restoration of the Jews to their own Land, in Connection with their Future Conversion . . . London, 1841.

M'NEILE, HUGH. Popular Lectures on the Prophecies Relative to the Jewish Nation. London, 1838. *Roth, B16/44.*

SEDGWICKE, WILLIAM. Zions Deliverance and her Friends Duty: or The Grounds of Expecting, and Meanes of Procuring Jerusalems Restauration . . . London, 1643. *Not in Roth.*

RICHARD BROTHERS

[Williams, Thomas] The Age of Credulity: A Letter to Nathaniel Brassey Halhed . . . in Answer to his Testimony in Favour of Richard Brothers, . . . London, 1795. *This London edition of B17/55 not in Roth. Pagination from second page of preface: 336–377.*

[BROTHERS, RICHARD] A Revealed Knowledge of the Prophecies and Times . . . Containing, with Other Great and Remarkable Things, Not Revealed to any other Person on Earth, the Restoration of the Hebrews to Jerusalem, by the Year 1798, under their Revealed Prince and Prophet. 2 parts in 1 volume. London, 1794. *Roth, B17/14.*

BRYAN, WILLIAM. A Testimony of the Spirit of Truth, concerning Richard Brothers . . . in an Address to the People of Israel, etc . . . London, 1795. *Roth, B17/21.*

HALHED, NATHANIEL BRASSEY. A Calculation on the Commencement of the Millennium, and a Short Reply to Dr. Horne's Pamphlet, Entitled, "Sound Argument, Dictated by Common Sense" . . . London, 1795. *Roth, B17/29.*

HALHED, NATHANIEL BRASSEY. A Revealed Knowledge of the Prophecies and Times [2 volumes] . . . To which is added, The Testimony of the Authenticity of the Prophecies of Richard Brothers, and of his Mission to Recall the Jews. Dublin, 1795. *Three volumes in one. This edition not in Roth.*

HALHED, NATHANIEL BRASSEY. The Speech of N.B.H., Esq., Delivered in the House of Commons . . . 1795, Respecting the Confinement of Mr. Brothers, the Prophet. London, 1795. *Not in Roth.*

HALHED, NATHANIEL BRASSEY. Testimony of the Authenticity of the Prophecies of Richard Brothers, and of his Mission to Recall the Jews. London, 1795. *Roth, B17/32.*

MOSER, JOSEPH. Anecdotes of Richard Brothers, in the Years 1791 and 1792, with some Thoughts upon Credulity, Occasioned by the Testimony of Nathaniel Brassey Halhed . . . London, 1795. *Roth, B17/39.*

PEREIRA, MOSES GOMEZ [pseudonym] The Jew's Appeal on the Divine Mission of Richard Brothers, and N. B. Halhed, Esq. to Restore Israel, and Rebuild Jerusalem . . . London, 1795. *Roth, B17/41.*

Prophéties de Jacques [sic] Brothers, ou la Connaissance révélée . . . Paris, IV (1796) *Not in Roth.*

ROTH, CECIL. The Nephew of the Almighty. An experimental account of the Life and Aftermath of Richard Brothers, R. N. London (1933) *Roth, A10/32.*

WILLIAMS [ELIZA] The Prophecies of Brothers Confuted from Divine Authority. London, 1795. *Roth, B17/53.*

WRIGHT, JOHN. A Revealed Knowledge of Some Things that will Speedily be Fulfilled in the World . . . London, 1794. *Roth, B17/16.*

MOSES HESS

HESS, MOSES. Ökonomische Schriften. Darmstadt, 1972.

BRAVO, GIAN MARIO. Il socialismo da Moses Hess alla Prima Internazionale nella recente storiografia. Torino, 1971.

By THEODOR HERZL

HERZL, THEODOR. Autograph (Alt-Aussee) 1901.

HERZL, THEODOR. Der Flüchtling. Lustspiel. Leipzig [1887]

HERZL, THEODOR. Das Palais Bourbon. Bilder aus dem französischen Parlamentsleben. Leipzig, 1895. *First edition.*

On THEODOR HERZL

ELON, AMOS. Herzl. New York, etc., 1975.

FUCHS, THEODOR. Festrede anlässlich des 71. Geburtstages Dr. Theodor Herzls gehalten . . . 1931. Wien (1931)

HAEZRAHI, YEHUDA. Theodor Herzl. Man of Vision and Reality. Jerusalem, 1954.

ISH-KISHOR, SULAMITH. How Theodor Herzl created the Jewish National Fund. New York (1960)

SCHNELLER, LUDWIG. Die Kaiserfahrt durchs Heilige Land. Leipzig, 1899.

STEWART, DESMOND. Theodor Herzl. Garden City, New York, 1974.

MAX NORDAU

NORDAU, MAX. Degenerazione. Torino, 1923.

NORDAU, MAX. Zeitgenössische Franzosen. Litteraturgeschichtliche Essays. Berlin, 1901.

NORDAU, MAX. Vierter Zionisten-Kongress. Bericht über den Zustand der Juden auf der ganzen Welt. No place [1900?]

NORDAU, MAX. The Malady of the Century. London, 1896. *Presentation copy. Inscribed and signed by the author.*

NORDAU, MAX. La malattia del secolo. Piacenza, 1914.

NORDAU, MAX. Le Menzogne Convenzionali della Nostra Civiltà. Milano, 1946.

NORDAU, MAX. Paradossi. Sesto S. Giovanni, 1913.

NORDAU, MAX. Paradossi. Piacenza, 1914.

NORDAU, MAX. Paradoxe. Leipzig, 1885. *First edition.*

NORDAU, MAX. Paradoxes psychologiques. Paris, 1896.

NORDAU, MAX. Parigi sotto la Terza Repubblica. Milano, 1881.

NORDAU, MAX. Seifenblasen. Federzeichnungen und Geschichten. Leipzig (Reclam) no date.

GALENO, GABRIELE (editor) Le menzogne convenzionali della nostra civiltà. Roma e Milano, 1950.

SHAW, BERNARD. The Sanity of Art: An Exposure of the Current Nonsense about Artists being Degenerate. London, 1911.

AHAD HA-AM

ACHAD HA-AM. Ten Essays on Zionism and Judaism. London, 1922.

ACHAD HA-AM. The Transvaluation of Values (1898) London, 1917.

Ahad Ha-Am, Prophet of Cultural Zionism. A Syllabus (editor, Kinereth Dushkin Gensler) New York, no date.

CHAIM WEIZMANN

WEIZMANN, CHAIM. The Letters and Papers of . . . Series A: Letters. Volume I. London, 1968.

WEIZMANN, CHAIM. Significati e metodi della ricostruzione Palestinese. Milano, 1930.

SIMON, LEON. Chaim Weizmann. Jerusalem, 1953.

YAHUDA, A. S. Dr. Weizmann's Errors On Trial. A Refutation of his Statements in "Trial and Error" Concerning my Activity for Zionism During my Professorship at Madrid University (New York) 1952.

Dr. Chaim Weizmann. Israels erster Staatspräsident. (Zum 75. Geburtstag des Präsidenten) Wien, 1949.

ARTHUR RUPPIN

RUPPIN, A. Die ersten Leistungen (Die landwirtschaftliche Kolonisationstätigkeit der Zionistischen Organisation) Jerusalem/London, 1935.

RUPPIN, ARTHUR. Memoirs, Diaries, Letters (editor, Alex Bein) London, 1972.

VLADIMIR JABOTINSKY

JABOTINSKY, VLADIMIR. Taryag Millim. 613 (Hebrew) Words. Introduction into Spoken Hebrew (in Latin Characters) New York (1949)

JABOTINSKY, VLADIMIR. Neue Zionistische Organisation (Prag, 1935)

BENARI, J. Vie et oeuvre de Zeev Vladimir Jabotinsky. Tunis, no date.

CHAIM ARLOSOROFF

ARLOSOROFF, CHAIM. Surveying American Zionism. New York (1929)

JUDAH L. MAGNES

MAGNES, JUDAH L. Russia and Germany at Brest-Litovsk. New York, 1919.

MAGNES, J. L. Reden des Kanzlers der Hebräischen Universität . . . zur Eröffnung des Studienjahres 1931–32 . . . Jerusalem, 1932.

MAGNES, J. L. Address of the President of the Hebrew University . . . at the Opening of the Academic Year 1938/39. Jerusalem, 1939.

CHAIM NACHMAN BIALIK

BIALIK, CH. N. Gedichte. Köln and Leipzig, 1911.

BIALIK, HAYIM NAHMAN. Halachah and Aggadah. London, 1944.

BIALIK, HAYIM NAHMAN. The Hebrew Book. An Essay. Jerusalem, 1951.

DAVID BEN GURION

BEN GURION, D[AVID] Autograph Letter Signed, 1 page. Sdeh Boker, September 30, 1963. To group of students at Matawan Regional High School, Matawan, New Jersey.

BEN GOURION, DAVID. Le peuple et l'état d'Israel. Paris, 1959.

LITVINOFF, BARNET. Ben-Gurion of Israel. London, 1954.

LOUIS D. BRANDEIS

BRANDEIS, LOUIS D. The Curse of Bigness. Miscellaneous Papers. New York, 1934.

RABINOWITZ, EZEKIEL. Justice Louis D. Brandeis. The Zionist Chapter of His Life. New York, 1968.

STERN, ELLEN NORMAN. Embattled Justice. The Story of Louis Dembitz Brandeis. Philadelphia, 1971.

TODD, A. L. Justice on Trial: The Case of Louis D. Brandeis. New York, etc., 1964.

TERRITORIALISM

RABINOWICZ, OSKAR K. New Light on the East Africa Scheme [London] 1952. *Offprint.*

STERN, DESIDER. Ein Kolonisationsplan für Juden. Prešov (Slovensko) 1939.

KARL MARX, *Bibliography*

Die Bibliothek des Instituts für Marxismus-Leninismus beim Zentralkomitee der SED. Ein Sammelband. Berlin, 1969.

DRAHN, ERNST. Das Archiv der Sozialdemokratischen Partei Deutschlands, seine Geschichte und Sammlungen. Gautzsch bei Leipzig, 1920.

Die Gemeinschaftsarbeiten von Marx und Engels. Eine Sammlung von Originalausgaben. Glashütten and Königstein im Taunus [1976]

Geschichte des Sozialismus in Erst- und Originalausgaben. Ausstellung ... 1926 ... Wien. Katalog. Zürich (1964) *Reprint of Wien, 1926.*

Marx Engels Verzeichnis. Zweiter Band. Briefe Postkarten Telegramme. Berlin, 1971.

STERN, HEINZ AND WOLF, DIETER. Das grosse Erbe. Eine historische Reportage um den literarischen Nachlass von Karl Marx und Friedrich Engels. Berlin, 1972.

UROYEVA, A. For All Time and All Men. Moscow, 1969.

KARL MARX, *Genealogy*

BRILLING, BERNHARD. Beiträge zur Geschichte der Juden in Trier. In: Trierisches Jahrbuch 1958. Trier, 1958.

ROSENSTEIN, NEIL. The Unbroken Chain. New York, 1976.

KARL MARX, *Letters*

REETZ, JÜRGEN. Vier Briefe von Jenny Marx aus den Jahren 1856–1860. Trier, 1970.

KARL MARX, *First Editions*

MARX, KARL. Der Achtzehnte Brumaire des Louis Bonaparte. Hamburg, 1869. *Second edition. First edition in book form. See Marx-Engels Erstausgaben, page 22.*

By KARL MARX

MARX, KARL AND ENGELS, FRIEDRICH. Scritti italiani (editor Gianni Bosio) Roma, 1972.

MARX, KARL AND ENGELS, FRIEDRICH. The Cologne Communist Trial. New York, 1971.

MARX, KARL. Surveys from Exile (Political Writings Volume II) New York, 1974.

MARX, KARL. The Grundrisse (editor David McLellan) New York, etc., 1972.

MARX ET ENGELS. Ecrits militaires. Paris, 1970.

(MARX, KARL) Le poesie epigrammatiche del giovane Karl Marx. Roma, 1968. *In: Carte segrete, anno II, n.5*

MARX, KARL. Betrachtung eines Jünglings bei der Wahl eines Berufes. Trier, 1947.

MARX, KARL. Kritik des Hegelschen Staatsrechts. Stuttgart, 1973.

MARX, KARL AND ENGELS, FREDERICK. The Revolution of 1848–49. Articles from the Neue Rheinische Zeitung. New York, 1972.

MARX, KARL. Der Bürgerkrieg in Frankreich. Berlin-Wilmersdorf, 1919.

MARX, KARL. The Class Struggles in France, 1848–1850 (translator, Henry Kuhn) Brooklyn, New York, 1967.

ENGELS, FRIEDRICH AND MARX, KARL. Reichsgründung und Kommune. Die Ereignisse von 1870–71 ... Berlin, 1920.

MARX, KARL AND ENGELS, FRIEDRICH. Staatstheorie. Frankfurt, etc., 1974.

MARX, KARL. Genesis of Capital. Moscow, 1969.

MARX, KARL AND ENGELS, FRIEDRICH. Zur Geschichte des Bundes der Kommunisten. Berlin, 1971.

MARX – LENIN. K židovské otázce. (Praha) 1932.

MARX, K. AND ENGELS, F. Materialismo storico e storiografia filosofica (editor Mario Dal Pra) Milano [1969]

MARX, CARLOS AND ENGELS, FEDERICO. Tesis sobre Feuerbach y otros escritos filosóficos. México, D.F., 1970.

MARX [AND OTHER AUTHORS] Marxismo e sindacato. Roma, 1970.

MARX, KARL AND ENGELS, FREDERICK. Articles on Britain. Moscow, 1971.

MARX, KARL AND ENGELS, FREDERICK. Ireland and the Irish Question. Moscow, 1971.

MARX, KARL AND ENGELS, FRIEDRICH. Die russische Kommune (editor Maximilian Rubel) München, 1972.

(MARX, KARL) Marx on China. Articles from the New York Daily Tribune 1853–1860. London, 1968.

MARX, ENGELS, LENIN. Über die Frau und die Familie. Leipzig, 1972.

MARX, KARL. Un chapitre inédit du Capital. Paris, 1971.

MARX, KARL AND ENGELS, FRIEDRICH. Über Deutschland und die deutsche Arbeiterbewegung. 2 volumes. Berlin, 1961–1970.

MARX, KARL AND ENGELS, FREDERICK. The Communist Manifesto with an introduction by Leon Trotsky. New York, 1970.

ENGELS, FRIEDRICH AND MARX, KARL. Reichsgründung und Kommune. Die Ereignisse von 1870–71 (editor A. Conrady) Berlin, 1920.

GODELIER, MARX, ENGELS. Sobre el modo de producción asiático. Barcelona, 1969.

KORSCH, K. AND MARX, K. Zur Geschichte der deutschen Arbeiterbewegung 1836–1875. Randglossen zum Gothaer Programm. No place, no date.

CERRONI, UMBERTO (editor) Il pensiero di Marx. Roma, 1975.

PIANCIOLA, CESARE (editor) Il pensiero di Karl Marx. Torino, 1971.

EASTON, LOYD D. AND GUDDAT, KURT H. (editors) Writings of the Young Marx on Philosophy and Society. New York, 1967.

ENZENSBERGER, HANS MAGNUS (editor) Gespräche mit Marx und Engels. 2 volumes. Frankfurt am Main, 1973.

On KARL MARX

ACTON, H. B. What Marx really said. New York, 1971.

ADELMANN, FREDERICK J. (editor) Demythologizing Marxism. A Series of Studies on Marxism. Boston and The Hague, 1969.

ALTHUSSER, LOUIS. Marxismus und Ideologie. Probleme der Marx-Interpretation. Westberlin, 1973.

ANSART, PIERRE. Marx e l'anarchismo. Bologna, 1972.

Apotegmas a propósito del marxismo con motivo de la conmemoración del nacimiento de Carlos Marx. No place, 1970.

ARNASON, JÓHANN PÁLL. Von Marcuse zu Marx. Prolegomena zu einer dialektischen Anthropologie. Neuwied and Berlin, 1971.

(AUTORENKOLLEKTIV) Aktuelle Bedeutung der Marxschen Randglossen zum Gothaer Programm. Berlin, 1976.

BACKHAUS, WILHELM. Marx, Engels und die Sklaverei. Düsseldorf, 1972.

BACKHAUS, WILHELM. Marx, Engels und die Sklaverei. Düsseldorf, 1974.

BAHR, H. D. [AND OTHERS] Anarchismus und Marxismus. Berlin, 1973.

BARTSCH, GÜNTER. Schulen des Marxismus. Troisdorf, 1970.

BECHER, HERBERT. Karl Marx und die Revolution von 1848. Berlin, 1953.

BECKER, WERNER. Kritik der Marxschen Wertlehre. Hamburg, 1973.

Beiträge zur Marx/Engels-Forschung. Berlin, 1968.

BIENERT, WALTHER. Der überholte Marx. Seine Religionskritik und Weltanschauung kritisch untersucht. Stuttgart, 1975.

BERNFELD, SIEGFRIED [AND OTHERS] Psychoanalyse und Marxismus. Dokumentation einer Kontroverse. Frankfurt am Main, 1970.

BIANCHI, MARINA. La teoria del valore dai classici a Marx. Bari, 1970.

BIOLAT, GUY. Marxisme et environnement. Paris, 1973.

BLOCH, ERNST [AND OTHERS] Marx und die Revolution. Frankfurt am Main, 1970.

BLUMENBERG, WERNER. Marx en documentos propios y testimonios graficos. Madrid, 1970.

BÖCKELMANN, FRANK. Über Marx und Adorno. Schwierigkeiten der spätmarxistischen Theorie. Frankfurt am Main, 1972.

BRACHT, WILHELM. Trier und Karl Marx (Trier) 1946.

BREITENBÜRGER, GERD AND SCHNITZLER, GÜNTER (editors) Marx und Marxismus heute. Hamburg, 1974.

BRÜGEL, FRITZ UND KAUTSKY, BENEDIKT (editors) Der deutsche Sozialismus von Ludwig Gall bis Karl Marx. Wien/Leipzig, 1931.

BRUHAT, JEAN. Karl Marx/Friedrich Engels. Essai biographique. Paris, 1970. *Limited numbered edition.*

BRUHAT, JEAN. Karl Marx/Friedrich Engels. Essai biographique (Paris) 1971.

BRUNHOFF, SUZANNE DE. La moneta in Marx. Roma, 1973.

BUHLE, PAUL. Marxismus in den USA. Berlin, 1974.

BUONFINO, GIANCARLO. La politica culturale operaia da Marx e Lassalle alla rivoluzione di Novembre 1859–1919. Milano, 1975.

BURIAN, WILHELM. Psychoanalyse und Marxismus. Eine intellektuelle Biographie Wilhelm Reichs. Frankfurt am Main, 1972.

CALICCIA, SANDRA. Lavoro, valore e prezzo nella teoria di Marx. Roma-Bari, 1973.

CARANDINI, GUIDO. Lavoro e capitale nella teoria di Marx. Padova, 1971.

CARLEBACH, JULIUS. Karl Marx and the Radical Critique of Judaism. London, etc., 1978.

CHROMUSCHIN, G. Der Marxismus und die sowjetische Ökonomik. Moskau, no date.

CLAUDIN, FERNANDO. Marx, Engels y la revolución de 1848. Mexico, etc., 1975.

COLLETTI, LUCIO. Marxismus als Soziologie. Berlin, 1973.

COMOTH, KATHARINA. Publizistische Elemente in der Lehre des jungen Marx. Berlin, 1970. *Dissertation.*

D'HONDT, JACQUES. De Hegel à Marx. Paris, 1972.

DICKMANN, JULIUS. Der Arbeitsbegriff bei Marx. Wien, 1932.

DOBB, MAURICE. On Marxism to-day. London, 1932.

DOGNIN, PAUL-DOMINIQUE. Introduzione a Karl Marx. Roma, 1972.

DOMARCHI, JEAN. Marx et l'histoire. Paris, 1972.

DRESSLER, HELMUT. Ärzte um Karl Marx. Berlin, 1970.

DURAND, PIERRE. La vie amoureuse de Karl Marx. Paris, 1970.

EDWARDS, THEODORE AND BONPANE, BLASE. Marxism and Christianity: Are They Compatible? A Debate. New York, 1970.

EGGERATH, WERNER. Marxismus und Arbeiterklasse. Weimar, 1948.

ERCKENBRECHT, ULRICH. Marx' Materialistische Sprachtheorie. Kronberg Ts., 1973.

Eretici del marxismo. Roma, 1970.

Ergebnisse und Perspektiven. Probleme der Praxis und Theorie des Marxismus. Berlin, no date.

Erklärungen und Kommentare zu: Karl Marx "Das Kapital." Münster, 1971.

ERTL, GEORG. Der gute Mensch von Trier. Karl Marx wie ihn niemand kennt. Köln, 1973.

EVANS, MICHAEL. Karl Marx. London, 1975.

FABBRI, L. Historische und sachliche Zusammenhänge zwischen Marxismus und Anarchismus. Berlin, 1972.

FALK, CURT. Karl Marx. Erzählt für unsere Jugend. Bodenbach, 1935.

FARACOVI, ORNELLA POMPEO. Il marxismo francese contemporaneo fra dialettica e struttura (1945–1968) Milano, 1972.

FAVRE, PIERRE ET MONIQUE. Les marxismes après Marx. Paris, 1970.

FEDOSEYEV, P. N. [AND OTHERS] Karl Marx. A Biography. Moscow, 1973.

FEDOSSEJEW, P. N. Der Marxismus im 20. Jahrhundert. Marx, Engels, Lenin und die Gegenwart. Berlin, 1973.

FISCHER, ERNST. Le marxisme véritable. Paris, 1972. *Avec la collaboration de Franz Marek.*

FLEISCHER, HELMUT. Marx und Engels. Die philosophischen Grundlinien ihres Denkens. München, 1970.

FONER, PHILIP (editor) When Karl Marx Died. New York, 1973.

FONTENAY, ELISABETH DE. Les figures juives de Marx. No place, 1973.

FROMM, ERICH. Marx e Freud. Milano, 1971.

FUCHS, EMIL. Von Schleiermacher zu Marx. Berlin (1969)

GARAUDY, ROGER. Clefs pour Karl Marx. Paris, 1964. *Title-page has only "Karl Marx."*

GARAUDY, ROGER. Introducción al estudio de Marx. México, 1970.

GEDÖ, ANDRÁS. Der entfremdete Marx. Berlin, 1971.

GODELIER, MAURICE AND SÈVE, LUCIEN. Marxismo e strutturalismo. Torino, 1970.

GONZALEZ-RUIZ, JOSÉ MARIA. Croire après Marx. Marxisme et christianisme devant l'homme nouveau. Paris, 1971.

GOUX, JEAN-JOSEPH. Freud, Marx: Économie et Symbolique. Paris, 1973.

GRAMSCI, ANTONIO. Marxisme als filosofie van de praxis. Amsterdam, 1972.

GRANDJONC, JACQUES. Marx et les communistes allemands à Paris 1844. Paris, 1974.

GRASSI, ERNESTO. Humanismus und Marxismus. Reinbek, 1973.

GROTEWOHL, OTTO. Gedankenkraft und Sprachgewalt bei Marx und Engels. Berlin, 1958.

GROTEWOHL, OTTO. Die geistige Situation der Gegenwart und der Marxismus. Berlin, 1948.

GRUJIĆ, PREDRAG M. Zur Ontologie des Marxismus. München, 1972.

GUHR, GÜNTER. Karl Marx und theoretische Probleme der Ethnographie. Berlin, 1969.

Guide to Marxist Philosophy. An Introductory Bibliography. Chicago, 1972.

GUIDUCCI, ROBERTO. Marx dopo Marx. Dalla rivoluzione industriale alla rivoluzione del terziario avanzato. No place, 1970.

GÜNTHER, HANS (editor) Marxismus und Formalismus. Dokumente einer literaturtheoretischen Kontroverse. München, 1973.

HANISCH, ERNST. Karl Marx und die Berichte der österreichischen Geheimpolizei. Trier, 1976.

HAUG, WOLFGANG FRITZ. Vorlesungen zur Einführung ins "Kapital." Köln, 1974.

HENRICH, FRANZ (editor) Humanismus zwischen Christentum und Marxismus. München, 1970.

HERRE, GÜNTHER. Verelendung und Proletariat bei Karl Marx. Düsseldorf, 1973.

HUNDT, MARTIN. Louis Kugelmann. Eine Biographie des Arztes und Freundes von Karl Marx und Friedrich Engels. Berlin, 1974.

HUNDT, MARTIN. Wie das "Manifest" entstand. Berlin, 1973.

JORDAN, Z. A. (editor) Karl Marx: Economy, Class and Social Revolution. London, 1972.

JOSHI, P. C. (editor) Homage to Karl Marx. A Symposium. Delhi, etc., 1969.

JUDIN, P. [and others] 100 Jahre "Manifest der Kommunistischen Partei". Berlin, 1948.

JULIER, ELMAR. Marx-Engels-Verfälschung und Krise der bürgerlichen Ideologie. Berlin, 1975.

KADENBACH, JOHANNES. Das Religionsverständnis von Karl Marx. München, etc., 1970.

KALIVODA, ROBERT. Marx et Freud. La pensée contemporaine et le marxisme. Paris, 1971.

KAMENKA, EUGENE. The Ethical Foundations of Marxism. London and Boston, 1972.

Der Kampf von Karl Marx und Friedrich Engels um die revolutionäre Partei der deutschen Arbeiterklasse. Berlin, 1977.

KAPP, YVONNE. Eleanor Marx. 2 volumes. New York, 1973–1976.

KEMPER, MAX. Marxismus und Landwirtschaft. Offenbach, 1973.

KISS, GABOR. Marxismus als Soziologie. Reinbek bei Hamburg, 1971.

KLIEM, MANFRED (editor) Karl Marx. Dokumente seines Lebens 1818 bis 1883. Leipzig, 1970.

KORSCH, KARL. Einführung in den Marxismus. Wunstorf, 1973.

KORSCH, K. AND MARX, K. Zur Geschichte der deutschen Arbeiterbewegung 1836–1875. Randglossen zum Gothaer Programm. No place, no date.

KORSCH, KARL. Die materialistische Geschichtsauffassung. Eine Auseinandersetzung mit Karl Kautsky. Leipzig, 1929.

KRADER, LAWRENCE. Ethnologie und Anthropologie bei Marx. München, 1973.

KRAMER, DIETER. Reform und Revolution bei Marx und Engels. Köln, 1971.

KRASSÓ, NICOLÁS AND MANDEL, ERNEST AND JOHNSTONE, MONTY. El marxismo de Trotski. Cordoba, 1970.

LAPIN, N. I. Der junge Marx. Berlin, 1974.

LAUER, QUENTIN AND GARAUDY, ROGER. Sind Marxisten die besseren Christen? Ein Streitgespräch. Hamburg, 1969.

LAUFNER, RICHARD AND KÖNIG, KARL-LUDWIG. Bruno Bauer, Karl Marx und Trier. Trier, 1978.

LAUFNER, RICHARD AND RAUCH, ALBERT. Die Familie Marx und die Trierer Judenschaft. Trier, 1975.

LEE, FRANZ JOHN TENNYSON. Der Einfluss des Marxismus auf die nationalen Befreiungsbewegungen in Südafrika. Frankfurt am Main, 1971.

LEHNING, ARTHUR. Anarchismus und Marxismus in der russischen Revolution [Also] [*Arthur Müller-Lehning*]

MAXIMOFF, G. P. Revolutionär-syndikalistische Bewegung in Russland. Berlin, 1971.

LESER, NORBERT. Die Odyssee des Marxismus. Auf dem Weg zum Sozialismus. Wien, etc., 1971.

LEWIS, JOHN. The Marxism of Marx. London, 1972.

LINDENBERG, DANIEL. Le marxisme introuvable (Paris) 1975.

LINK, CHRISTIAN. Theologische Perspektiven nach Marx und Freud. Stuttgart, etc., 1971.

LÖBL, EUGEN. Marxismus – Wegweiser und Irrweg. Wien and Düsseldorf, 1973.

LOPEZ, DAVIDE. Analisi del carattere ed emancipazione: Marx, Freud, Reich. Milano, 1970.

LÖWENSTEIN, JULIUS I. Vision und Wirklichkeit. Marx contra Marxismus. Basel and Tübingen, 1970.

LOWY, MICHAEL. La théorie de la révolution chez le jeune Marx. Paris, 1970.

LUPERINI, ROMANO. Marxismo e letteratura. Bari, 1971.

LUPORINI, CESARE. Karl Marx-Kommunismus und Dialektik. Frankfurt am Main and Köln, 1974.

LYOTARD, JEAN-FRANÇOIS. Dérive à partir de Marx et Freud. Paris, 1973.

McLELLAN, DAVID. Karl Marx. His Life and Thought. New York, etc., 1973.

McLELLAN, DAVID. The Thought of Karl Marx. An Introduction. London, etc., 1971.

MAGNO, GINO. I profeti della protesta. Marx . . . Milano, 1971.

MAGUIRE, JOHN. Marx's Paris Writings: an analysis. Dublin, 1972.

MALEWSKY-MALEWITSCH, SWJATOSLAV V. Auf Marx wird Rabatt gegeben. Osnabrück, 1973.

MAN, HENRI DE. Au delà du marxisme. Bruxelles, 1927.

MANDEL, ERNEST. The Formation of the Economic Thought of Karl Marx 1843 to Capital. New York and London, 1971.

MANDEL, ERNEST. The Marxist Theory of the State. New York, 1969.

MARCUSE, HERBERT AND SCHMIDT, ALFRED. Existenzialistische Marx-Interpretation. Frankfurt am Main, 1973.

MÁRKUS, GYÖRGY. La teoria della conoscenza nel giovane Marx. Saggio sui manoscritti del 1844. Milano, 1971.

MARRAMAO, GIACOMO. Marxismo e revisionismo in Italia. Bari, 1971.

Karl Marx 5. Mai 1818–14. März 1883 Ein Material zur Ausgestaltung von Karl-Marx-Feiern (Dresden, 1953)

Karl Marx 1818/1968. Bad Godesberg, 1968. *Various authors.*

KARL-MARX-HAUS TRIER. Bilddokumente über das Geburtshaus von Karl Marx in Vergangenheit und Gegenwart. Trier, 1977.

Marxismus und Anarchismus. Theorie-Kritik-Praxis. Berlin, 1973.

Marxismus Archiv. Band I. Marxismus und Politik. Frankfurt am Main, 1971.

Marxismusstudien. Siebte Folge. Tübingen, 1972.

MASCITELLI, ERNESTO. Il marxismo e la funzione della cultura. Milano, 1972.

MATTICK, PAUL. Marx and Keynes. The Limits of the Mixed Economy. Boston, 1969.

MATTICK, PAUL. Marx und Keynes. Die Grenzen des "gemischten Wirtschaftssystems." Frankfurt and Wien, 1971.

MAUKE, MICHAEL. Die Klassentheorie von Marx und Engels. Frankfurt am Main, 1970.

MAZUMDAR, SATYENDRA NARAYAN. Marxism and the Language Problem in India. New Delhi, etc., 1970.

MAZZETTI, ROBERTO. Il feticismo di Marx o la fine di una illusione. Roma, 1972.

MELOTTI, UMBERTO. Marx. Firenze, 1974.

MELOTTI, UMBERTO. Marx e il terzo monde. Milano, 1972.

MERKEL, RENATE. Marx und Engels über Sozialismus und Kommunismus. Zur Herausbildung der Auffassung von Karl Marx und Friedrich Engels über die sozialistische und kommunistische Gesellschaft in der Entstehungsperiode des wissenschaftlichen Kommunismus (1842–1846) Berlin, 1974.

MÉSZÁROS, ISTVÁN. Marx's Theory of Alienation. London, 1970.

MEYER, THOMAS. Der Zwiespalt in der Marx'schen Emanzipationstheorie. Kronberg Ts., 1973.

MILIBAND, RALPH. Marx und der Staat. Berlin, 1971.

MIRANDA, JOSÉ PORFIRIO. Marx y la Biblia. Critica a la filosofia de la opresión. Salamanca, 1972.

MISRAHI, ROBERT. Marx et la question juive. Paris, 1972.

MONDOLFO, RODOLFO. Umanismo di Marx. Studi filosofici 1908–1966. Torino, 1968.

MÖNKE, WOLFGANG. Die heilige Familie. Zur ersten Gemeinschaftsarbeit von Karl Marx und Friedrich Engels. Berlin, 1972.

MONZ, HEINZ. Karl Marx. Grundlagen der Entwicklung zu Leben und Werk. Trier, 1973.

MONZ, HEINZ. Karl Marx – Trierer Reminiszenzen. Trier, 1969.

MONZ, HEINZ [AND OTHERS] Der unbekannte junge Marx. Neue Studien zur Entwicklung des Marxschen Denkens 1835–1847. Mainz, 1973.

MONZ, HEINZ [AND OTHERS] Zur Persönlichkeit von Marx' Schwiegervater Johann Ludwig von Westphalen. Trier, 1973.

MORAWSKI, STEFAN. Il marxismo e l'estetica. Roma, 1973.

MÜLLER-HERLITZ, URSULA. Karl Marx: Wesen und Existenz des Menschen. München, 1972.

NAPOLEONI, CLAUDIO. Lezioni sul Capitolo sesto inedito di Marx. Torino, 1972.

NAPOLEONI, CLAUDIO. Smith Ricardo Marx. Considerazioni sulla storia del pensiero economico. Torino, 1970.

NEGRI, ANTONIO. Zyklus und Krise bei Marx. Berlin, 1972.

Nieder mit dem Marxismus! [Switzerland, no date]

NIEL, HENRI. Karl Marx. Situation du Marxisme. Paris, 1971.

NIEL, MATHILDE. Psychoanalyse des Marxismus. München, 1972.

NOVACK, GEORGE. An Introduction to the Logic of Marxism. New York, 1969.

NOVACK, GEORGE. Marxism versus Neo-Anarchist Terrorism. New York, 1970.

OLGIATI, FRANCISCO. Carlos Marx. Buenos Aires, 1950.

OLLIVIER, MARCEL. Marx et Engels poètes. Paris, 1933.

ORFEI, RUGGERO. Marxismo e umanesimo. Roma, 1970.

OSBORN, REUBEN [pseudonym of REUBEN OSBERT] Marxism and Psycho-Analysis. London, 1965.

PADOVER, SAUL K. Karl Marx. An Intimate Biography. New York, etc., 1978.

PAILLET, MARC. Marx contre Marx. La société technobureaucratique. Paris, 1971.

PAPAIOANNOU, KOSTAS. Marx et les Marxistes. Paris, 1972.

PARETO, VILFREDO. Marxisme et économie pure. Genève, 1966.

PARKINSON, C. NORTHCOTE. Good-bye, Karl Marx. Hamburg, 1970.

PASSALACQUA, GIUSEPPE. Marx giovane a Praga. Roma [1962]

PAYNE, ROBERT. The Unknown Karl Marx. New York, 1971.

PETROVIĆ, GAJO. Philosophie und Revolution. Modelle für eine Marx-Interpretation. Reinbek bei Hamburg, 1971.

PONOMARJOW, B. N. Das "Manifest der Kommunistischen Partei" und die Gegenwart. Berlin, 1973.

PORTER, THOMAS W. (editor) An Interview with Karl Marx in 1879 (first published in the Chicago Tribune . . . 1879) New York, 1972.

Psychoanalyse Marxismus und Sozialwissenschaften. s'Gravenhage, 1971.

QUINIOU, JEAN CLAUDE. Marxismus und Informatik. Berlin, 1974.

RABEHL, BERND. Geschichte und Klassenkampf. Einführung in die marxistische Geschichtsbetrachtung der Arbeiterbewegung. Berlin, 1973.

RACKWITZ, ARTHUR. Der Marxismus im Lichte des Evangeliums. Untersuchungen über das Kommunistische Manifest. Berlin, 1948.

RADDATZ, FRITZ J. Karl Marx. Eine politische Biographie. Hamburg, 1975.

RANCIÈRE, JACQUES. Der Begriff der Kritik und die Kritik der politischen Ökonomie von den "Pariser Manuskripten" zum "Kapital." Berlin, 1972.

REICH, W. AND SAPIR, I. AND FROMM, E. Psicoanalisi e marxismo. Roma, 1972.

REICHELT, HELMUT. Zur logischen Struktur des Kapitalbegriffs bei Karl Marx. Frankfurt and Wien, 1970.

Revue internationale de Philosophie. Number 45–46 [Special fascicle:] Karl Marx. Bruxelles, 1958.

RJAZANOV, D. Marx und Engels nicht nur für Anfänger. Berlin, 1973.

RODRIGUEZ-LORES, J. Die Grundstruktur des Marxismus. Gramsci und die Philosophie der Praxis. Frankfurt am Main, 1971.

ROVATTI, PIER ALDO. Critica e scientificità in Marx. Milano, 1973.

SANDKÜHLER, HANS JÖRG. Praxis und Geschichtsbewusstsein. Studie zur materialistischen Dialektik, Erkenntnistheorie und Hermeneutik. Frankfurt am Main, 1973.

SCHAFF, ADAM. Marx oder Sartre? Versuch einer Philosophie des Menschen. Berlin, 1965.

SCHAFF, ADAM. Strukturalismus und Marxismus. Essays. Wien, 1974.

SCHLEIFSTEIN, JOSEF. Einführung in das Studium von Marx, Engels und Lenin. München, 1972.

SCHLOSSER, HERTA. Marxismus und Religion. Die politische Interpretation des Religiösen in der DDR . . . Meisenheim am Glan, 1970.

SCHWAN, GESINE. Die Gesellschaftskritik von Karl Marx. Stuttgart, etc., 1974.

SCHWERIN VON KROSIGK, LUTZ GRAF. Jenny Marx. Liebe und Leid im Schatten von Karl Marx. Wuppertal, 1976.

SEIFFERT, HELMUT. Marxismus und bürgerliche Wissenschaft. München, 1971.

SEN, MOHIT AND RAO, M. B. (editors) Das Kapital Centenary Volume. A Symposium. Delhi, etc., 1968.

SHAW, WILLIAM H. Marx's Theory of History. Stanford, California, 1978.

SIMON, BRIAN (editor) The Challenge of Marxism. London, 1963.

SLOAN, PAT. Marx and the Orthodox Economists. Oxford, 1973.

SPINELLA, MARIO (editor) Marx vivo. La presenza di Karl Marx nel pensiero contemporaneo. 2 volumes (Roma) 1969.

STADLER, PETER. Karl Marx. Ideologia e politica. Roma, 1971.

STEFFEN, GUSTAF F. Den materialistiska samhällsuppfattningens historia före Karl Marx. Stockholm, 1914.

STEPANOVA, E. Karl Marx. Short Biography. Moscow, 1968.

STREY, JOACHIM AND WINKLER, GERHARD. Marx und Engels 1848/49. Die Politik und Taktik der "Neuen Rheinischen Zeitung" während der bürgerlich-demokratischen Revolution in Deutschland. Berlin, 1972.

STRUIK, DIRK J. (editor) Birth of the Communist Manifesto. New York, 1971.

SUSLOV, MIKHAIL. Karl Marx – Brilliant Teacher and Leader of the Working Class. Moscow, 1970.

TERRAY, EMMANUEL. Marxism and "Primitive" Societies. New York and London, 1972.

THOMAS, TONY. Marxism versus Maoism. A Reply to the "Guardian." New York, 1974.

(TROTZKY) Marx vu par Trotzky. Paris, 1970.

TRUMER, M. Le matérialisme historique chez K. Marx et Fr. Engels. Paris, 1933. *Dissertation.*

TRU'O'NG-CHINH. Forward along the Path Charted by K. Marx. Hanoi, 1969.

TSCHUDI, LORENZ. Rätedemokratie und Marxismus. Basel, 1972.

ULBRICHT, WALTER. Die Bedeutung des Werkes "Das Kapital" von Karl Marx für die Schaffung des entwickelten gesellschaftlichen Systems des Sozialismus in der DDR . . . Berlin, 1967.

VACCA, GIUSEPPE. Marxismo e analisi sociale. Bari, 1969.

VARDYS, V. STANLEY (editor) Karl Marx Scientist? Revolutionary? Humanist? Lexington, Massachusetts, etc., 1971.

WACKENHEIM, CHARLES. La faillite de la religion d'après Karl Marx. Paris, 1963.

WALTER, E. O. Marxismus oder Bolschewismus. Olten (1919)

WETTE, WOLFRAM. Kriegstheorien deutscher Sozialisten. Marx, Engels, Lassalle, Bernstein,

Kautsky, Luxemburg. Ein Beitrag zur Friedensforschung. Stuttgart, etc., 1971.

WETTER, GUSTAV A. Der dialektische Materialismus. Seine Geschichte und sein System in der Sowjetunion. Wien, 1956.

WEYMANN, ANSGAR. Gesellschaftswissenschaften und Marxismus. Düsseldorf, 1972.

WILLIAMS, RAYMOND. Marxism and Literature. Oxford, etc., 1977.

ZETKIN, KLARA. Karl Marx und sein Lebenswerk! Vortrag . . . Elberfeld (1913)

MARX: ENGELS

ENGELS, FRIEDRICH. Cola di Rienzi. Ein unbekannter dramatischer Entwurf (editor, Michael Knieriem) Trier, 1974.

ENGELS, F. AND LENIN, W. I. Militärpolitische Schriften. 2 volumes. Berlin, 1930–31.

FRIEDRICH ENGELS LEBEN UND WERK. Ausstellung. Düsseldorf (1970) *Exhibition catalogue.*

ANDRÉAS, BERT. Unbekanntes und Vergessenes von Friedrich Engels. Hannover, 1971. *Offprint.*

PELGER, HANS AND KNIERIEM, MICHAEL. Friedrich Engels als Bremer Korrespondent . . . Trier, 1975.

PELGER, HANS AND KNIERIEM, MICHAEL. Friedrich Engels als Bremer Korrespondent . . . Trier, 1976.

WESSEL, HARALD. Hausbesuch bei Friedrich Engels. Eine Reise auf seinem Lebensweg. Berlin, 1971.

MARX: AVELING

FLAUBERT, GUSTAVE. Madame Bovary [Translated by Eleanor Marx Aveling] London, 1952. *See Tsuzuki, Life of Eleanor Marx 1855–1898 (Oxford, 1967), page 166, but omitted on page 341.*

HASTINGS, MICHAEL. Tussy is me. A romance. London, 1970.

KAPP, YVONNE. Eleanor Marx. Volume I, Family Life (1855–1883) New York, 1973.

WESSEL, HARALD. Tussy oder siebenundzwanzig Briefe über das sehr bewegte Leben von Eleanor Marx-Aveling . . . Leipzig (1975)

MARX: FIRST INTERNATIONAL

BRAVO, GIAN MARIO. Il socialismo da Moses Hess alla Prima Internazionale nella recente storiografia. Torino, 1971

Documents of the First International. The General Council of the First International 1864–1872. Minutes. 5 volumes. Moscow, no date.

MARX: COMMUNE

MARX, KARL. Der Bürgerkrieg in Frankreich. Berlin-Wilmersdorf, 1919.

MARX, KARL AND LENIN, V. I. The Civil War in France: The Paris Commune. New York, 1968.

MARX, KARL AND ENGELS, FREDERICK. On the Paris Commune. Moscow, 1971.

MARX, KARL AND ENGELS, FRIEDRICH. Tagebuch der Pariser Kommune. Berlin, 1971.

MARX: BAKUNIN

DUCLOS, JACQUES. Bakounine et Marx. Ombre et lumière. (Paris) 1974.

KOCH, GERD. Marx und Bakunin zur Pariser Kommune: Zerstört den Staat! Hamburg, 1974.

MÜLLER, HANS. Michael Bakunin. Der revolutionäre Anarchismus. Zürich, 1919.

MARX: MEHRING

MEHRING, FRANZ. Herr Hofprediger Stöcker der Socialpolitiker. Eine Streitschrift. Bremen, 1882.

MEHRING, FRANZ. Herrn Hardens Fabeln. Berlin, 1899.

MEHRING, FRANZ. Storia della Democrazia Sociale Tedesca. Parte prima (1830–1863) Roma, 1900.

MEHRING, FRANZ. Über den historischen Materialismus. Berlin, 1947.

LINDAU, RUDOLF. Franz Mehring zu seinem 100. Geburtstag ... 1946. Berlin (1946)

MARX: KAUTSKY

KAUTSKY, KARL. Elsass-Lothringen. Stuttgart, 1917.

KAUTSKY, KARL. Die Internationalität und der Krieg. Berlin, 1915.

KAUTSKY, KARL. Thomas More und seine Utopie. Stuttgart, 1888.

KAUTSKY, KARL. Die proletarische Revolution und ihr Programm. Berlin and Stuttgart, 1922.

KAUTSKY, KARL. Der Ursprung des Christentums. Stuttgart, 1921.

KAUTSKY, KARL. Wie der Weltkrieg entstand. Berlin, 1919.

Die Gesellschaft. Internationale Revue für Sozialismus und Politik. Sonderheft: Karl Kautsky dem Wahrer und Mehrer der Marx'schen Lehre zum 70. Geburtstage. Berlin (1924)

KORSCH, KARL. Die materialistische Geschichtsauffassung. Eine Auseinandersetzung mit Karl Kautsky. Leipzig, 1929.

MARX: BUKHARIN

BUCHARIN UND SINOWJEW. Der neue Kurs. Reden der Genossen Bucharin und Sinowjew. Brief des Ekki. Berlin, 1925.

BUCHARIN, N. Vom Sturze des Zarismus bis zum Sturze der Bourgeoisie. Hamburg, 1971. *Reprint of: Berlin, 1919.*

MARX: LENIN

LENIN, W. I. Über die Judenfrage. Moskau, 1932.

LENIN, W. I. Über die Judenfrage. Wien-Berlin, 1932.

LENIN. On the Jewish Question. New York, 1934.

LENIN. On the Jewish Question (editor, Hyman Lumer) New York, 1974.

LENIN, V. I. Carlos Marx. Federico Engels. Moscú, no date.

LENIN, V. I. Karl Marx and His Teachings. Moscow, 1973.

LENIN, V. I. Marxism and Revisionism. Moscow, 1969.

LENIN, V. I. Marxism on the State. Preparatory Material for the Book The State and Revolution. Moscow, 1972.

Lenins Werk in deutscher Sprache. Bibliographie. Berlin, 1967.

ANDREWS, R. F. (editor) What Lenin said about the Jews. Extracts from His Writings [London] no date.

SOCIALISM AND THE JEWISH QUESTION

HASS, ERIC. Socialism Answers Anti-Semitism. New York, 1944.

[HASS, ERIC] Socialism Answers Anti-Semitism. Brooklyn, New York, 1971.

LÉON, ABRAHAM. Judenfrage und Kapitalismus. München, 1973.

MOHRMANN, WALTER. Antisemitismus. Ideologie und Geschichte im Kaiserreich und in der Weimarer Republik. Berlin, 1972.

SEIDMAN, PETER. Socialists and the Fight Against Anti-Semitism. An Answer to the B'nai B'rith Anti-Defamation League. New York, 1973.

JEWISH SOCIALISTS

ABRAMOWITSCH, MARK. Hauptprobleme der Soziologie (Probleme marxistischer Lebenserkenntnis) Berlin, 1930.

ABUSCH, ALEXANDER. Stalin und die Schicksalsfragen der deutschen Nation. Berlin, 1949.

AUSTERLITZ, FRIEDRICH. Von Schwarzrotgold bis Schwarzgelb. Was die Deutschradikalen waren und was sie sind! Wien, 1911.

BAUER, OTTO. Der Balkankrieg und die deutsche Weltpolitik. Berlin, 1912.

BAUER, OTTO. Der Genfer Knechtungsvertrag und die Sozialdemokratie. Rede . . . Wien, 1922.

BAUER, OTTO. Nationaler Kampf oder Klassenkampf? Ein Gespräch. Wien, 1911.

BAUER, OTTO. Krieg und Friede in den Gewerkschaften? Wien, 1910.

BAUER, OTTO. Die Nationalitätenfrage und die Sozialdemokratie. Wien, 1907.

BAUER, OTTO. Schulreform und Klassenkampf. Wien, 1921.

BAUER, OTTO. Die Teuerung. Eine Einführung in die Wirtschaftspolitik der Sozialdemokratie. Wien, 1910.

BAUER, OTTO. Der Übergang vom Kapitalismus zum Sozialismus (Wien) 1962.

BAUER, OTTO. Das Weltbild des Kapitalismus. Frankfurt am Main, 1971.

(BAUER, OTTO) Nach der deutschen Katastrophe. Die Beschlüsse der Internationalen Konferenz der S.A.I. in Paris . . . 1933, und die Rede des Berichterstatters Otto Bauer. Zürich, 1933.

[*Bauer, Otto*] KUN, BÉLA. Otto Bauers Weg. Von der Anerkennung des Ständestaates – zur Anerkennung der Diktatur des Proletariats. No place, 1934.

BORN, STEPHAN. Erinnerungen eines Achtundvierzigers. Leipzig, 1898. *Name originally Simon Buttermilch.*

BRAUN-VOGELSTEIN, JULIE. Was niemals stirbt. Gestalten und Erinnerungen. Stuttgart, 1966.

BRAUNTHAL, JULIUS. Auf der Suche nach dem Millenium. 2 volumes. Nürnberg, 1948–1949.

DEUTSCH, JULIUS. Die Geschichte der sozialistischen Gewerkschaften Oesterreichs bis zur Krise des Jahres 1873. Wien, 1907. *Dissertation.*

DEUTSCH, JULIUS. Die Tarifverträge in Oesterreich. Wien, 1908.

DEUTSCH, JULIUS. Treueid und Revolution. Eine Rede vor Gericht. Wien, 1923.

DEUTSCH, JULIUS. Schwarzgelbe Verschwörer. Wien, 1925.

DEUTSCH, JULIUS. Ein weiter Weg. Lebenserinnerungen. Zürich, etc., 1960. *See Leo Baeck Year Book Volume* XVI, *page 110.*

DEUTSCH, JULIUS. Wehrmacht und Sozialdemokratie. Berlin, no date.

DEUTSCHER, ISAAC. On Socialist Man. New York, 1969.

DEUTSCHER, ISAAC. Die unvollendete Revolution 1917–1967. Anhang: Der Verlauf der Revolution 1917. Frankfurt am Main, 1967.

FECHENBACH, FELIX. Im Haus der Freudlosen. Bilder aus dem Zuchthaus. Berlin, 1925.

FRANK, LUDWIG. Die bürgerlichen Parteien des Deutschen Reichstags Stuttgart, 1911.

FRANK, LUDWIG. Reden, Aufsätze und Briefe (editor, Hedwig Wachenheim) Berlin, no date.

GRUNBERGER, RICHARD. Red Rising in Bavaria. London, 1973.

HILFERDING, RUDOLF. Die Aufgaben der Sozialdemokratie in der Republik [Rede] auf dem Parteitag zu Kiel . . .1927 (Berlin, 1927)

[*Hilferding*] PIETRANERA, GIULIO. R. Hilferding und die ökonomische Theorie der Sozialdemokratie. Berlin, 1974.

KISCH, EGON ERWIN. Eintritt verboten. Paris, 1934.

[*Koestler, Arthur*] KANAPA, JEAN. Le Traitre et le Prolétaire ou l'entreprise Koestler and co. ltd. suivi d'inédits sur les procès de Mathias Rakosi. Paris, 1950.

KREISKY, BRUNO. Die Herausforderung. Politik an der Schwelle des Atomzeitalters. Wien, etc., 1963.

[*Kreisky*] LENDVAI, PAUL AND RITSCHEL, KARL HEINZ. Kreisky. Porträt eines Staatsmannes. Wien, etc., 1972.

[*Kreisky*] SPECTATOR (pseudonym) Mann auf Draht. Bruno Kreisky. Wien, no date.

[*Kugelmann*] HUNDT, MARTIN. Louis Kugelmann. Eine Biographie des Arztes und Freundes von Karl Marx und Friedrich Engels. Berlin, 1974.

[*Kun, Bela*] BIZONY, LADISLAUS. 133 Tage ungarischer Bolschewismus. Die Herrschaft Béla Kuns und Tibor Szamucllys Die blutigen Ereignisse in Ungarn. Leipzig/Wien, 1920.

[*Kun, Bela*] GÁL, IRÉN. Béla Kun. Roma, 1969.

[*Kun, Bela*] HERCZEG, GÉZA. Béla Kun. Eine historische Grimasse. Berlin, 1928.

[*Laski, Harold*] MARTIN, KINGSLEY. Harold Laski (1893–1950) a biographical memoir. London, 1953.

LEVI, PAUL. Unser Weg. Wider den Putschismus. Mit Anhang: Die Lehren eines Putschversuches von Karl Radek. Berlin, 1921.

LEVI, PAUL. Wehrhaftigkeit und Sozialdemokratie. Berlin, no date.

[*Leviné*] MEYER-LEVINÉ, ROSA. Leviné. Leben und Tod eines Revolutionärs. Erinnerungen. München, 1972.

[*Leviné*] SLONIMSKI, M. Eugen Leviné. Erzählung. Berlin, 1949.

LIPMAN, NATHAN. Mit der Roten Armee im Fernen Osten. Aufzeichnungen eines Rotarmisten. Moskau, 1932.

LUKÁCS, GEORG. Fortschritt und Reaktion in der deutschen Literatur. Berlin, 1950.

LUKÁCS, GEORG. Wissenschaftliche Intelligenz, Schulung, Organisationsfrage. Frühe Aufsätze 1919–1921. No place, no date. *Originally: Löwinger.*

LUKÁCZ, GEORG. Alte und neue Kultur. No place, 1970. *Reprint of Wien, 1921.*

LUKÁCS, GEORG. Methodisches zur Organisationsfrage (Neuwied and Berlin, 1968)

LUKÁCS, GEORG. Schicksalswende. Beiträge zu einer neuen deutschen Ideologie. Berlin, 1948.

LUKÁCS, GEORG. Die Zerstörung der Vernunft. Berlin, 1954.

Georg Lukács zum 13. April 1970 (Goethepreis '70) Neuwied and Berlin, 1970.

[*Lukács*] ALTHAUS, HORST. Georg Lukács oder Bürgerlichkeit als Vorschule einer marxistischen Ästhetik. Bern and München, 1962.

[*Lukács*] BAHR, EHRHARD. La pensée de Georg Lukács. Toulouse, 1972.

[*Lukács*] LICHTHEIM, GEORGE. Georg Lukács. München, 1971.

[*Lukacs*] In Memory of Georg Lukacs. Chicago, 1971.

[*Martow*] Julius Martow. Sein Werk und seine Bedeutung für den Sozialismus. Berlin, 1924.

MODIGLIANI, [VITTORIO EMANUELE] Dalla guerra alla rinnovazione socialista. Milano, 1919.

NEURATH, OTTO. Wesen und Weg der Sozialisierung. München, 1919.

[*Parvus-Helphand*] SCHARLAU, WINFRIED B. AND ZEMAN, ZBYNĚK A. Freibeuter der Revolution. Parvus-Helphand. Eine politische Biographie. Köln, 1964.

POPOFF, GEORGE. Ich sah die Revolutionäre. Moskauer Erinnerungen und Begegnungen während der Revolutionsjahre. Bern, 1967.

[*Rajk*] L'Affaire Rajk. Compte rendu sténographique complet des Séances du Tribunal du Peuple, à Budapest... 1949. (Paris) 1949.

RÁKOSI, MÁTYÁS. Rede... und Diskussionsrede von Imre Nagy... am 11. Juli 1953 (Budapest, 1953) *Speech by Nagy not contained in volume.*

[*Rákosi, Mátyás*] KONKOLY, KÁLMÁN. Das Geheimnis des Mátyás Rákosi. Eine Fibel des Weltkommunismus. Wien-Köln, 1962.

[*Rákosi, Mátyás*] Mátyás Rákosi. Sein Leben in Bildern. Budapest, 1952.

RAPPOPORT, CHARLES. Le Marxisme est-il périmé? Paris, 1933.

RAPPOPORT, CHARLES. La révolution sociale (Encyclopédie Socialiste... de l' Internationale Ouvrière) Paris, 1912.

RAPPOPORT, CHARLES. Pourquoi nous sommes socialistes? (Encyclopédie Socialiste... de l'Internationale Ouvrière) Paris, 1913.

[*Rosselli*] SALVEMINI, GAETANO. Carlo e Nello Rosselli. Paris, no date.

SENDER, TONI. The Autobiography of a German Rebel. New York, 1939.

[*Slansky*] Prozess gegen die Leitung des staatsfeindlichen Verschwörerzentrums mit Rudolf Slánský an der Spitze (Prag) 1953.

[*Slansky*] LONDON, ARTHUR. Ich gestehe. Der Prozess um Rudolf Slansky. Hamburg, 1970.

STAMPFER, FRIEDRICH. Erfahrungen und Erkenntnisse. Aufzeichnungen aus meinem Leben. Köln, 1957.

STAMPFER, FRIEDRICH. Die vierzehn Jahre der ersten deutschen Republik. Hamburg, 1947.

SZÁNTÓ, BÉLA. Klassenkämpfe und die Diktatur des Proletariats in Ungarn (Mit einem Vorwort von Karl Radek) Wien [1920]

VERGELIS, ARON. On the Jewish Street. Travel Notes. Moscow, 1971.

VERGELIS, AARON. Letters from Europe (January-March 1971) Moscow, 1972.

WACHENHEIM, HEDWIG. Vom Grossbürgertum zur Sozialdemokratie. Memoiren einer Reformistin. Berlin, 1973.

By FERDINAND LASSALLE

LASSALLE, FERDINANDO. L'agitazione dell'Unione Generale Operaia Germanica e le promesse del Re di Prussia (1864) Roma, 1904.

[LASSALLE, FERDINAND] Arbeiterlesebuch. Rede Lassalle's zu Frankfurt am Main . . . 1863. Leipzig, no date. *Fifth edition.*

LASSALLE, FERDINAND. Assisen-Rede gehalten . . . zu Düsseldorf . . . 1849 . . . Leipzig, 1870.

(LASSALLE, FERDINAND) Intime Briefe Ferdinand Lassalles an Eltern und Schwester (editor, Eduard Bernstein) Berlin, 1905. *Andréas, B27.*

LASSALLE, FERD. Erwiderung auf eine Recension der Kreuz-Zeitung über das Buch Herr Bastiat-Schulze aus Delitzsch . . . Leipzig, 1872.

LASSALLE, FERDINANDO. Forza e diritto. Lettera aperta (1863) Roma, 1907.

LASSALLE, F. Macht und Recht. Leipzig, 1870. *Second edition.*

LASSALLE, FERDINANDO. Per la questione operaia. Discorso . . . 1863 (1863) Roma, 1903.

LASSALLE, F. Die Philosophie Fichte's und die Bedeutung des Deutschen Volksgeistes. Berlin, 1862. *First edition.*

Il processo per alto tradimento contro Ferdinando Lassalle (12 Marzo 1864) Roma, 1909.

(LASSALLE, FERDINANDO) Il processo dinanzi alla Corte d'Appello di Düsseldorf . . . 1864 (1866) Roma, 1908.

LASSALLE, FERDINAND. Reden und Schriften/ Tagebuch/ Seelenbeichte . . . nebst einer Darstellung seines Lebens und Wirkens. (editor, Hans Feigl) Wien, 1920.

LASSALLE, FERDINAND. Ueber Verfassungswesen. Leipzig, 1873. *Fifth edition.*

On FERDINAND LASSALLE

BECKER, BERNHARD. Geschichte der Arbeiter-Agitation Ferdinand Lassalle's. Hildesheim, 1972. *Reprint of: Braunschweig, 1874.*

KEGEL, MAX. Ferdinand Lassalle. Gedenkschrift zu seinem 25 jährigen Todestag. Stuttgart, 1890. *Andréas, C84.*

PLENER, ERNST VON. Ferdinand Lassalle. Leipzig, 1884. *Andreas, C167.*

RACOWITZA, HÉLÈNE DE. Princesse et Comédienne. Souvenirs de ma vie. Paris, no date.

ROSENBAUM, EDUARD. Ferdinand Lassalle. Studien über historischen und systematischen Zusammenhang seiner Lehre. Jena, 1911.

UEXKÜLL, GÖSTA V. Ferdinand Lassalle in Selbstzeugnissen und Bilddokumenten. Reinbek, 1974.

ROSA LUXEMBURG

LUXEMBURG, ROSA. Die Akkumulation des Kapitals. Berlin, 1913. *First edition.*

LUXEMBURG, ROSA. Briefe an Leon Jogiches. Frankfurt am Main, 1971.

LUXEMBURG, ROSA U.A. Briefe an Mathilde Jacob (1913-1918) Tokio, 1972.

LUXEMBURG, ROSA. Internationalismus und Klassenkampf. Die polnischen Schriften (editor, Jürgen Hentze) Neuwied and Berlin, 1971.

LUXEMBURG, ROSA. Kirche und Sozialismus. Frankfurt am Main, no date.

LUXEMBOURG, ROSA-MEHRING, F. Polémique avec Vandervelde. Grèves sauvages. Spontanéité des masses. L'expérience belge de grève générale. Paris (1973) *Bound with Schwarz, Salomon: Lenine et le mouvement syndical, Paris (1973)*

LUXEMBURG, ROSA. Social Reform or Revolution. 1900. Colombo, Ceylon, 1969.

ADLER, MAX. Karl Liebknecht und Rosa Luxemburg. Gedenkworte. Wien, 1919.

BERADT, CHARLOTTE (editor) Rosa Luxemburg im Gefängnis. Briefe und Dokumente aus den Jahren 1915-1918. Frankfurt am Main, 1973.

CLIFF, TONY [pseudonym of YIGAL GLUCKSTEIN] Studie über Rosa Luxemburg. Frankfurt am Main, 1969.

GERAS, NORMAN. The Legacy of Rosa Luxemburg. London, 1976.

GUÉRIN, DANIEL. Rosa Luxemburg et la spontanéité révolutionnaire (Paris) 1971.

HERBIG, ERNA (editor) Karl Liebknecht – Rosa Luxemburg. Zum 100. Geburtstag. Anschauungsmaterial. Berlin, 1971.

HETMANN, FREDERIK (pseudonym of HANS CHRISTIAN KIRSCH) Rosa L. Die Geschichte der Rosa Luxemburg und ihrer Zeit. Weinheim and Basel, 1976.

LASCHITZA, ANNELIES AND RADCZUN, GÜNTER. Zum Wirken Rosa Luxemburgs in der revolutionären Arbeiterbewegung. Berlin, 1971. *In: Beiträge zur Geschichte der Arbeiterbewegung, 13/2.*

LASCHITZA, ANNELIES AND RADCZUN, GÜNTER. Zum Wirken Rosa Luxemburgs in der deutschen Arbeiterbewegung in den Jahren der ersten Revolution in Russland. Berlin, 1971. *In: Zeitschrift für Geschichtswissenschaft, XIX/4.*

LASCHITZA, ANNELIES AND RADCZUN, GÜNTER. Rosa Luxemburg. Ihr Wirken in der deutschen Arbeiterbewegung. Berlin, 1971.

Lenin – Rosa Luxemburg. Analyse ihrer Differenzen. Göttingen, 1971.

OSSOWSKI, JACEK. Rosa Luxemburg. Eine Streitschrift. Frankfurt, 1971.

Rosa Luxemburg und die Oktoberrevolution 1917. Hamburg, 1970.

SCHIEL, ILSE (editor) Karl und Rosa. Erinnerungen. Zum 100. Geburtstag von Karl Liebknecht und Rosa Luxemburg. Berlin, 1971.

SCHMIDT, GISELHER. Spartakus. Rosa Luxemburg und Karl Liebknecht. Frankfurt am Main, 1971.

WINKEL, UDO. Rosa Luxemburg und die deutsche Sozialdemokratie. Gaiganz, 1974.

LÉON BLUM

BLUM, LÉON. Bolchevisme et Socialisme. Paris, 1936.

BLUM, LÉON. Du mariage. Paris, 1937.

BLUM, LÉON. Radicalisme et Socialisme. Paris, 1936.

BLUM, LÉON. Dein Weg zum Sozialismus. Hamburg, 1947.

COLTON, JOEL. Léon Blum. Humanist in Politics. New York, 1966.

EDUARD BERNSTEIN

BERNSTEIN, ED. Die verschiedenen Formen des Wirtschaftslebens. Berlin, 1909.

BERNSTEIN, EDUARD. Die englische Gefahr und das deutsche Volk. Berlin, 1911.

BERNSTEIN, EDUARD. Die Internationale der Arbeiterklasse und der europäische Krieg. Tübingen, 1915.

BERNSTEIN, EDUARD. Wie eine Revolution zugrunde ging. Stuttgart, 1921.

BERNSTEIN, EDUARD. Wie ist wissenschaftlicher Socialismus möglich? Berlin, 1901.

BERNSTEIN, EDUARD. Völkerrecht und Völkerpolitik. Berlin, 1919.

BERNSTEIN, EDUARD. Von 1850 bis 1872. Kindheit und Jugendjahre. Berlin, 1926.

BERNSTEIN, EDUARD. Wirtschaftswesen und Wirtschaftswerden. Berlin, 1920.

COLLETTI, LUCIO. Bernstein und der Marxismus der Zweiten Internationale. Frankfurt am Main, 1971.

VICTOR AND FRIEDRICH ADLER

ADLER, FRIEDRICH. Die Besetzung des Ruhrgebietes und die Internationale. Wien, 1923.

ADLER, FRIEDRICH. Das Stalinsche Experiment und der Sozialismus. Wien, 1932.

Friedrich Adler. Zum achtzigsten Geburtstag [Wien, 1959]

ADLER, VICTOR. Die Marodeure des Klerikalismus. Rede . . . Wien, 1901.

KOCMATA, KARL F. Dr. Viktor Adler und die österreichische Arbeiterbewegung. Wien, 1920.

KURT EISNER

EISNER, KURT. Treibende Kräfte. Berlin, 1915.

EISNER, KURT. Der Sozialismus und die Jugend. Basel, 1919.

LEONARD NELSON

NELSON, LEONARD. Vom Beruf der Philosophie unserer Zeit für die Erneuerung des öffentlichen Lebens. Leipzig, 1918.

NELSON, LEONARD. Über wissenschaftliche und ästhetische Naturbetrachtung. Berlin, no date.

DANIEL DE LEON

DE LEON, DANIEL. Capitalism Means War. Brooklyn, New York, 1970.

DE LEON, DANIEL. Capitalism vs. Socialism. Brooklyn, New York, 1969.

DE LEON, DANIEL. Socialist vs. Capitalist Economics (Marx on Mallock) New York, 1963.

DE LEON, DANIEL. Flashlights of the Amsterdam Congress. New York, 1929.

DE LEON, DANIEL. Die Prinzipien-Erklaerung der I.W.W. . . . Braunschweig, 1920.

PETERSEN, ARNOLD. Daniel De Leon. Emancipator. New York, 1946.

PETERSEN, ARNOLD. Daniel De Leon. Internationalist. New York, 1948.

PETERSEN, ARNOLD. Daniel De Leon. Pioneer Socialist Editor. Brooklyn, New York, 1966.

PETERSEN, ARNOLD. Daniel De Leon. Social Scientist. New York, 1945.

PETERSEN, ARNOLD. Ein Gegner ohne Ehre. New York, 1958.

REEVE, CARL. The Life and Times of Daniel De Leon. New York, 1972.

EMMA GOLDMAN

GOLDMAN, EMMA. The Traffic in Women and other essays on feminism. New York, 1970.

GOLDMAN, EMMA. Voltairine de Cleyre. Berkeley Heights, New Jersey, 1932. *Limited, numbered presentation copy.*

DRINNON, RICHARD. Rebel in Paradise. A Biography of Emma Goldman. Chicago, 1961. *Presentation copy signed by Drinnon.*

ISHILL, JOSEPH. Emma Goldman. A Challenging Rebel. Berkeley Heights, New Jersey, 1957. *Private edition. Presentation copy.*

SHULMAN, ALIX. To the Barricades. The Anarchist Life of Emma Goldman. New York, 1971.

By LEON TROTSKY

TROTSKY, L. Letter Signed, 1 page. Büyükada, January 6, 1931. To Herr Boni concerning arrangements for the publication of his "History of the Russian Revolution."

TROTZKY, N. Die Beilis-Affäre [Berlin] 1913. *In: Die Neue Zeit, 28 November 1913.*

TROTSKY, LEON. Class and Art. Problems of Culture under the Dictatorship of the Proletariat. London, 1968.

TROTSKY, LÉON. Classe ouvrière, syndicats, comité et parti. Paris, 1973.

TROTSKY, LEON. The Crisis of the French Section [1935–36] New York, 1977.

TROTSKY, LEON. The Death Agony of Capitalism and the Tasks of the Fourth International. The Transitional Program. New York, 1970.

TROTSKY, LEON. Europe and America: Two Speeches on Imperialism. New York, 1971.

TROTSKY, LEON. Fascism what it is and how to fight it. New York, 1969.

TROTSKY, LEON. On the Jewish Question. New York, 1970.

TROTSKY, LEON. After the July Days What Next? (August-September 1917) Colombo (Ceylon) 1967.

TROTZKI, LEO. Kommunismus oder Stalinismus? (Ausgewählte Schriften Nummer 1) [Berlin, 1971]

TROTSKY, LEON. The Young Lenin. Harmondsworth, etc., 1974.

TROTSKY, LEON. On Literature and Art (editor, Paul N. Siegel) New York, 1970.

(TROTZKY) Marx vu par Trotzky. Paris, 1970.

TROTSKY, LEON. Marxism in Our Time. New York, 1970.

TROTZKI, LEO. Wie wird der Nationalsozialismus geschlagen? Auswahl aus "Schriften über Deutschland." Frankfurt am Main, 1971.

TROTSKY, LEON. On the Paris Commune. New York, 1970.

TROTSKY, LEON. Portraits Political and Personal. New York, 1977.

TROTSKY, LEV. Premesse oggettive della rivoluzione socialista (Roma, 1970)

TROTSKY, LEON. Problems of Civil War. New York, 1970.

TROTSKY, LEÓN. El Programa de Transicion para la Revolucion Socialista. Caracas (Venezuela) 1973.

TROTSKIJ, L. D. Il programma di transizione. Roma, 1972.

TROTSKY, LEON. 1905. Results and Perspectives. Colombo (Ceylon) (1954)

TROTZKI, LEO. Revolution und Bürgerkrieg in Spanien 1931–39. 2 volumes. Frankfurt am Main, 1975-1976.

TROTSKY, LEON. The Chinese Revolution. Problems and Perspectives. New York (1969)

TROTSKI, LEÓN. La Revolucion China. México, D.F., 1970.

TROTZKI, LEO D. Die russische Revolution. Kopenhagener Rede 1932 [Also] SCHNEIDER, MICHAEL. Stalin oder Trotzki? Berlin, 1970.

TROTZKI, LEO. Schriften zur revolutionären Organisation. Reinbek bei Hamburg, 1970.

TROTSKY, LEON. For a Free Independent Soviet Ukraine! Toronto, 1974.

TROTSKY, LEON. Stalinism and Bolshevism. Concerning the historical and theoretical roots of the Fourth International. New York, 1970.

TROTSKY, LÉON. Nos tâches politiques (Paris, 1971)

TROTSKY, LEON. Tasks before the Twelfth Congress of the Russian Communist Party [1923] London, 1975.

TROTSKY, LEON. Against Individual Terrorism. New York, 1974.

TROTSKY, LEON. On the Suppressed Testament of Lenin. New York, 1970.

TROTZKI, L. Der Todeskampf des Kapitalismus und die Aufgaben der 4. Internationale (Übergangsprogramm) Berlin, 1972.

TROTSKY, LEON. On the Trade Unions. New York, 1975.

MEIJER, JAN M. (editor) The Trotsky Papers 1917-1922. 2 volumes. The Hague, etc., 1964, 1971.

TROTSKY, LEON. The War and the International 1915 . . . No place, 1971.

RYKOW AND TROTZKY, L. Die Wirtschaft in Sowjetrussland und in Westeuropa. Zusammenbruch und Wiederaufbau. Berlin, 1920.

TROTSKY, LEON. Women and the Family. New York, 1970.

TROTSKY, LEON. Women and the Family. New York, 1972. *Second edition.*

TROTSKY, LEON, Writings. 7 volumes. New York, 1969–1972. *1932–33, 1933–34 (1972); 1934–35 (1971); 1935–36, 1937–38 (1970); 1938–39, 1939–40 (1969)*

LOVELL, SARAH (editor) Leon Trotsky Speaks. New York, 1972.

MARX, KARL AND ENGELS, FREDERICK. The Communist Manifesto with an introduction by Leon Trotsky. New York, 1970.

On LEON TROTSKY

ABOSCH, HEINZ (editor) Trotzki-Chronik. Daten zu Leben und Werk. München, 1973.

American Trotskyism, 1928–1970 (New York) 1971. *New York University Libraries. Bulletin of the Tamiment Library, Number 47, April, 1971.*

AVENAS, DENISE AND BROSSAT, ALAIN. De l'Antitrotskysme. Éléments d'histoire et de théorie. Paris, 1971.

AVENAS, DÉNISE. Economia e politica nel pensiero di Trotskij. Roma, 1972.

AVENAS, DENISE. Trotzkis Beitrag zum Marxismus. Hamburg, 1972.

AVENAS, DENISE. Trotzkis Marxismus. Ökonomik und Politik in der Theorie Trotzkis. Frankfurt am Main, 1975.

The Bolshevik Party's Struggle Against Trotskyism (1903–February 1917) Moscow, 1969. *By various authors.*

The Bolshevik Party's Struggle Against Trotskyism in the Post-October Period. Moscow, no date.

CANNON, JAMES P. Leon Trotsky. Memorial Address "To the Memory of the Old Man." New York (1940)

CARMICHAEL, JOEL. Trotsky's Agony. London, 1972. *In: Encounter, May and June, 1972.*

CARMICHAEL, JOEL. Trotsky: An Appreciation of his Life. New York, 1975.

CORVISIERI, SILVERIO. Trotskij e il comunismo italiano. Roma, 1969.

FIGUÈRES, LÉO. O trotskismo. Lisboa, 1971.

GERMAIN, ERNEST. Leon Trotsky. The man and his action. Calcutta, no date.

GIORDANO, ALBERTO. Trotski la vita il pensiero i testi esemplari. Milano, 1972.

GORKIN, JULIAN. L'assassinat de Trotsky. Paris, 1970.

HEIJENOORT, JEAN VAN. With Trotsky in Exile. From Prinkipo to Coyoacán. Cambridge, Massachusetts and London, 1978.

HOWE, IRVING. Leon Trotsky. New York, 1978.

HUHN, WILLY. Trotzki – der gescheiterte Stalin. Berlin, 1973.

KRASSÓ, NICOLÁS AND MANDEL, ERNEST AND JOHNSTONE, MONTY. El marxismo de Trotski. Córdoba, 1970.

KRASSÓ, NICÒLAS (editor) Trotsky. The Great Debate Renewed. Saint Louis, Missouri, 1972.

LEVINE, ISAAC DON. Die Psyche des Mörders. Der Mann, der Trotzki tötete. Wien, etc., 1970.

LUMER, HYMAN. The Fight Against Trotskyism. New York [1971?]

MAVRAKIS, KOSTAS. Trotskismo: teoria e storia. Milano, 1972.

MOSLEY, NICHOLAS. The Assassination of Trotsky. London, 1972.

NEDAVA, JOSEPH. Trotsky and the Jews. Philadelphia, 1972.

OGURTSOV, SERGEI. The True Face of Neo-Trotskyism. Moscow, 1973.

PLUET, JACQUELINE. Trotski et le trotskisme. Paris, 1971.

PONOMARYOV, B. Trotskyism – A Weapon of Anti-Communism. An Urgent Task of Ideological and Political Struggle. Moscow, 1972.

SORLIN, PIERRE AND IRÈNE. Lénine; Trotski; Staline – 1921–1927. Paris, 1961.

Against Trotskyism. The Struggle of Lenin and the CPSU against Trotskyism. A Collection of Documents. Moscow, 1972.

WEISS, PETER. Trotsky in Exile. A Play. New York, 1972.

WILDE, HARRY. Trotski. Madrid, 1972.

WYNDHAM, FRANCIS AND KING, DAVID. Trotsky a documentary. Harmondsworth, etc., 1972.

LEON TROTSKY, *Moscow Trials*

Prozessbericht über die Strafsache des sowjetfeindlichen trotzkistischen Zentrums verhandelt . . . 1937 . . . Moskau, 1937.

Prozessbericht über die Strafsache des antisowjetischen "Blocks der Rechten und Trotzkisten" verhandelt … 1938 … Moskau, 1938.

SEDOW, LEO. Rotbuch über den Moskauer Prozess. Trotzkis Sohn berichtet. Hamburg, 1972. *Reprint of: Antwerpen, no date.*

GRIGORII ZINOVIEV

[*Sinowjew*] BUCHARIN AND SINOWJEW. Der neue Kurs. Reden der Genossen Bucharin und Sinowjew. Brief des Ekki. Berlin, 1925.

ZINOVIEV, GREGORY. Lenin. Speech to the Petrograd Soviet … 1918. London, 1966.

KARL RADEK

RADEK, KARL. Les Voies de la Révolution Russe. Paris, 1971.

LEVI, PAUL. Unser Weg. Wider den Putschismus. Mit Anhang: Die Lehren eines Putschversuches von Karl Radek. Berlin, 1921.

SZÁNTÓ, BÉLA. Klassenkämpfe und die Diktatur des Proletariats in Ungarn (Mit einem Vorwort von Karl Radek) Wien [1920]

GOLDBACH, MARIE-LUISE. Karl Radek und die deutsch-sowjetischen Beziehungen 1918–1923. Bonn-Bad Godesberg, 1973.

PAWEL, ERNST. Karl Radek – A Forgotten Pillar of Bolshevism [New York] 1972. *Offprint.*

OTHER SOVIET LEADERS

JAROSLAWSKY, EMIL. Religion und KP(B)RB. Moskau and Pokrowsk, 1926.

MAISKY, I. The Munich Drama. Moscow, 1972.

PJATNIZKI, O. Probleme der internationalen Gewerkschaftsbewegung. Moskau-Leningrad, 1935.

[*Swerdlow*] SWERDLOWA, KLAWDIJA. Jakow Michailowitsch Swerdlow. Erinnerungen an einen Kampfgefährten Lenins. Berlin, 1965.

YAROSLAVSKY, E. Landmarks in the Life of Stalin. London, 1942.

JEWISH QUESTION

Antisemitismus – eine erbliche Belastung. Kurzgefasster und volkstümlich gehaltener Nachweis. Von einem Wiener Kommunallehrer. Wien, 1913.

ARENDT, HANNAH. Antisemitism. New York (1968)

BARROSO, GUSTAVO. Judaismo, Maçonaria e Comunismo. Rio de Janeiro, 1937.

BLITZ, SAMUEL. Nationalism. A Cause of Anti-Semitism. New York, 1928.

BLOCH, JOCHANAN. Das anstössige Volk. Über die weltliche Glaubensgemeinschaft der Juden. Heidelberg, 1964.

BÖHM, FRANZ. Antisemitismus (Vortrag) (München, 1958)

BORCHSENIUS, POUL. Hep! Hep! Af antisemitismens historie. København, 1960.

ECKER, JAKOB. Der "Judenspiegel" im Lichte der Wahrheit. Eine wissenschaftliche Untersuchung. Paderborn, 1884.

ELIOT, GEORGE [pseudonym of MARY ANN EVANS] Die Juden und ihre Gegner. Hamburg, 1880.

EMANUEL. Das Rätsel "Judentum" Basel, 1944.

FÉRENZY, OSCAR DE. Os Judeus e nós os Christãos. São Paulo, etc., 1939.

GINIEWSKI, PAUL. Le point de vue Juif. Bruxelles, 1970.

GRAU, RUDOLF FRIEDRICH. Semiten und Indogermanen in ihrer Beziehung zu Religion und Wissenschaft. Stuttgart, 1864.

GRIMSTAD, BILL (editor) The Jews on Trial: Testimony of 330 Historic Figures on Jewry (Washington, District of Columbia, 1973)

HAHN, JULIUS. Die Judenfrage. Hamburg, 1922.

HERTZBERG, ARTHUR. Anti-Semitism and Jewish Uniqueness Ancient and Contemporary. Syracuse, 1975.

IZECKSOHN, ISAAC. O anti-semitismo: uma alergia social. São Paulo, 1954.

JONGE M[ORRIS] DE. Jeschuah, der klassische jüdische Mann. Zerstörung des kirchlichen, Enthüllung des jüdischen Jesus-Bildes. Berlin, 1904.

K. (PFR. in Dr. bei M.) Die jüdische und die christliche Moral. Leipzig, 1895. *Freimann, page 407.*

KESSLER, HARRY L. Jews and World Affairs. A Study in Current Jewish Events. New York, 1939.

KLEIN, S. Das Judenthum oder die Wahrheit über den Talmud. Basel, 1860.

KOOLE, J. L. De Joden in de verstrooiïng. Franeker [about 1940]

KURTH, PAUL. Arier und Juden. 2 volumes. Charlottenburg [1924]

LANDMANN, SALCIA. Die Juden als Rasse. Das Volk unter den Völkern. Olten and Freiburg im Breisgau, 1967.

Lee, J. Fitzgerald. The Great Migration. The Origin of the Jewish People and Materials towards the Solution of a World Problem. London, 1933.

Lendvai, Paul. Antisemitismus ohne Juden. Entwicklungen und Tendenzen in Osteuropa. Wien, 1972.

Leroy-Beaulieu, Anatole. L'antisémitisme. Paris, 1897.

Lovsky, F. Antisémitisme et mystère d'Israel. Paris, 1955.

Lublinski, S. Die Entstehung des Judentums. Eine Skizze. Berlin, 1903.

Luckner, Gertrud (editor) Beiträge zur christlichen Betrachtung der Judenfrage. Freiburg im Breisgau, 1951.

Luzsénszky, Br. A. Der Talmud in nichtjüdischer Beleuchtung. 5. Heft. Budapest, 1933.

Mignot, Pierre. Le problème Juif et le principe des nationalités. Paris [1923]

Mohrmann, Walter. Antisemitismus. Ideologie und Geschichte im Kaiserreich und in der Weimarer Republik. Berlin, 1972.

Nyström, Anton. Judarne förr och nu samt judefragan i östra Europa och dess lösning. Stockholm, 1919.

Oefele, Armin von. Reizliteratur. Semitische und andere Geheimnisse in Spenglers Pseudowissenschaft. München (1922)

Oppenheim, James. A Psycho-Analysis of the Jews. Girard, Kansas, 1926.

Osman-Bey. Gli ebrei alla conquista del mondo. Venezia, 1880.

O'Wickedone, P. R. Emporgepeitscht! Einschmelzen oder Totschlagen? Germania Gouvernante bei Israels? Zur arisch-jüdischen Pantomime. Zürich, 1898.

Parkes, James. The Conflict of the Church and the Synagogue. A Study in the Origins of Antisemitism. New York, 1969.

Parkes, James. The Jewish Question. Oxford, 1941.

Pesci, Ernesto. Lotta e destino di razza. Saggio d'interpretazione biologica. Terni, 1939 – XVII.

Pranaitis, I. B. Christianus in Talmude Iudaeorum sive Rabbinicae Doctrinae de Christianis secreta . . . Petropolis, 1892.

Rappaport, Ernest A. Anti-Judaism. A Psychohistory. Chicago, 1975.

Rathbone, Eleanor. F. Falsehoods and Facts about the Jews. London, 1944.

Richter, Arthur. Die Juden und wir. Marburg an der Lahn, 1962.

Ros, A. van. De Jood. Een waarschuwend woord aan den Christen. Roermond, 1891.

Sartre, Jean-Paul. Betrachtungen zur Judenfrage. Psychoanalyse des Antisemitismus. Zürich, 1948.

Schreiner, Martin. Die jüngsten Urteile über das Judentum. Berlin, 1902.

Jüdische Sitten-Gesetze (Auszug aus dem Talmud und Schulchan Aruch) Lorch (Württemberg) 1922.

Strack, Hermann L. Jüdische Geheimgesetze? Berlin, 1920.

Tal, Uriel. Religious and Anti-Religious Roots of Modern Anti-Semitism. New York, 1971.

Zenker, Ernst Victor. Mysticismus, Pietismus, Antisemitismus am Ende des neunzehnten Jahrhunderts. Wien, 1894.

RITUAL MURDER

Balaban, Majer. Hugo Grotius und die Ritualmordprozesse in Lublin (1636) Berlin, 1930. *Offprint.*

[Baumgarten, Emanuel] Die Blutbeschuldigung gegen die Juden. Von christlicher Seite beurtheilt. Wien, 1883.

Seiden, Morton Irving. The Paradox of Hate. A Study in Ritual Murder. South Brunswick, etc., 1967.

Stauf von der March, Ottokar. Der Ritualmord. Beiträge zur Untersuchung der Frage. Wien, 1933.

Semper, Willy. Kirche und Staat in Oesterreich. Neues zur Polna-Affaire (New York, 1902)

Schnitzer, H. Zwei Predigten vor und nach dem Tisza-Eszlarer Prozess gehalten. Budapest, 1883.

Trotzky, N. Die Beilis-Affäre [Berlin] 1913. *In: Die Neue Zeit, 28. November 1913.*

PROTOCOLS OF THE ELDERS OF ZION

Bergmeister, Karl. Der jüdische Weltverschwörungsplan. Die Protokolle der Weisen von Zion vor dem Strafgerichte in Bern. Erfurt, 1937.

Blacas, Jules. Sous l'étreinte juive. Paris (1936)

La Conspiration Juive contre les Peuples. "Protocols" Procès-verbaux de réunions secrètes des Sages d'Israël. Paris, 1920.

Die Entlarvung der Weisen von Zion. Von? (Die Bücher vom siegenden Kreuz) I. Teil: Die grosse Weltlüge. Berlin, no date. *About 1927.*

FREIRE, JOÃO PAULO (MÁRIO) Os Judeus e os protocolos dos sábios de Sião. 4 volumes. Lisboa, 1937–1939.

FRIEDRICH, OTTO. Die Weisen von Zion. Das Buch der Fälschungen. Lübeck (1920)

L'Internazionale Ebraica. I "Protocolli" dei "Savi Anziani" di Sion. Roma, 1937–XV.

Are All Jews Liars? [Open letter to] Dr. Abram Leon Sacher, Champaign, Illinois [*sic*] Tompkins Corners, New York, 1940.

Der Jüdische Kriegsplan zur Aufrichtung der Judenweltherrschaft im Jahre des Heils 1925. Nach den Richtlinien der Weisen von Zion. Lorch [1925]

LANGER, FELIX. Die Protokolle der Weisen von Zion. Rassenhass und Rassenhetze. Wien, 1934.

PONCINS, LÉON DE. La mystérieuse internationale juive. Paris, 1936.

RETCLIFFE, JOHN [pseudonym of HERMANN GOEDSCHE] Dr. Faust's Abenteuer auf dem Judenkirchhof in Prag und hernach. Lorch (1925)

RETCLIFFE, JOHN [pseudonym of HERMANN GOEDSCHE] Auf dem Judenkirchhof in Prag. Berlin, 1933.

CONVERTS AND CONVERSIONISM I, *to 1850*

BEIBITZ, JOSEPH. An Inhabitant of the Rock. Manchester, etc., 1844.

BICKERSTETH, E. The Restoration of the Jews to their own Land, in Connection with their Future Conversion . . . London, 1841.

CAPADOCE, A. Overdenkingen over Israels Roeping en Toekomst. Amsterdam, 1845.

[*Capadose*] [LAURIA, C. L.] Bekeering van Doctor A. Capadose, Portugeesch Israëliet . . . Amsterdam, 1845.

CARBEN, VICTOR VON. Ein schön vnd seüberlich Tractat von der edlen reinen vnd vnbefleckten junckfrawschafft Marie der hymelischen Künigin . . . Durch mich V. v. C. vor zeyten ein Jud vnd Rabi der Jüdischen geschrifft, vnd nun nach Christenlicher ein armer vnwürdiger Priester. Strassburg, 1519.

CLEVE, H. B. H. Der Geist des Rabbinismus, oder mein Uebertritt vom Juden- zum Christenthume. Münster, 1823.

FEHRE, SAMUEL BENJAMIN. Versuch einer Abhandlung von der noch bevorstehenden merkwürdigen Bekehrung der Juden . . . Schneeberg and Leipzig, 1753. *Eichstädt, 2224.*

FREY, JOSEPH SAMUEL C. F. A New Edition of a Hebrew Grammar, Considerably Altered, and Much Enlarged. New York, 1823. *Rosenbach, 238.*

FREY, JOSEPH SAMUEL C. F. A Hebrew Grammar in the English Language. London, 1839. *Roth, B15/52.*

GAZZOLI, GIACOMO M. (DI MODONA [Modena] GIA MAESTRO E PREDICATORE EBREO, EPOI CATTOLICO ROMANO) L'Ebreo disingannato. No date [18th century] *Manuscript.*

H., J. A. [i.e., JOHANN AUGUST HAUSMEISTER] Worte der Liebe an meine Brüder nach dem Fleisch, die Kinder Israel. Strassburg, 1838. *Eichstädt, 2302*

Hebrew Customs; or the Missionary's Return. Philadelphia [1834] *Rosenbach, 374.*

The Jewish Expositor, and Friend of Israel: Containing, Monthly Communications Respecting the Jews, and the Proceedings of the London Society. Volume I – 1816. London, 1816.

[MARKS, DAVID] The Life of David Marks, to the 26th year of his age. Including the particulars of his conversion, call to the ministry . . . Written by himself. Limerick, Maine, 1831. *This edition not in Rosenbach.*

MEDICI, PAOLO SEBASTIANO. . . . Midolla della lingua santa ovvero breve metodo per imparar facilmente la Lingua Ebraica . . . Firenze, 1694.

MEDICI, PAULO. Promptuarium Biblicorum textuum ad catholicam, fidem confirmandam et Judaeorum infirmandam perfidiam. Florentiae, 1707. *Fürst II, page 338.*

[MEDICI, PAOLO SEBASTIANO] Selva delle radici ebraiche e delle voci che più remotamente da esse procedono. Firenze, 1694. *See H. Szancer, The exotic Medici (Flushing, New York, 1964), page 17 and note 14.*

MEDICI, PAOLO. Riti, e costumi degli Ebrei . . . Venezia, 1781.

MEDICI, VITALE. Omelie fatte alli Ebrei di Firenze nella Chiesa di Santa Croce, et sermoni fatti in piu compagnie della detta città. Firenze, 1585. *See H. Szancer, The exotic Medici, Flushing, New York, pages 5–6.*

[*Moses the Jew*] The Substance of Three Sermons, Preached at Edinburgh . . . 1787, by Moses the Jew, Who was lately converted to the Christian Religion . . . [Edinburgh?] 1812. *Roth, B6/100.*

[MOZZI, MARCANTONIO] Lettere ad un amico sopra certa dissertazione pubblicata in Brescia sul ritorno degli Ebrei alla Chiesa. Lucca, 1777.

MYERS, ALFRED MORITZ. The History of a Young Jew . . . Chester, 1840. *Roth, A10/22.*

PHELPS, SAMUEL M. The Triumphs of Divine Grace, a Poem . . . A Description of the Millennial Reign of Jesus Christ on Earth, by a Converted Israelite. New York, 1835.

PRIESTLEY, JOSEPH. Letters to the Jews; Inviting them to an Amicable Discussion of the Evidences of Christianity. Birmingham, 1787. *Second edition with Part II added. Roth, B4/23.*

RAABIUS, CHRISTOPHORUS THEOPHILUS. Dissertatio theologica de mysterio conversionis Iudaicae gentis ante mundi finem . . . Giessae, 1716.

[*Ratisbonne*] Die wunderbare Bekehrung des Israeliten, Herrn Alphons Ratisbonne in Rom . . 1842. Nach zuverlässigen . . . Nachrichten bearbeitet von einem katholischen Geistlichen. Aachen, 1842.

Relation de la Ceremonie du Batême de deux jeunes Juifs, Faite dans l'Eglise Metropolitaine Saint Etienne de Toulouse . . . 1732 (Toulouse, 1732)

[SAMUEL MAROCHITANUS] Tractatus Rabby Samuelis, errorem Iudeorum indicans. Brescia, 1535.

[SAMUEL MAROCHITANUS] Rabbi Samuelis Tractatus, indicans errorem Iudaeorum . . . Antwerpiae, 1711.

[*Samuel Marochitanus*] AMINTA, FILIPPO. L'ebraisimo [*sic*] senza replica e sconfitto colle stesse sue armi . . . Roma, 1823.

SCHUBERT, JOHAN ERNST. Schriftmäsige Gedanken von der algemeinen Jüdenbekehrung und dem Tausendjärigen Reich. Jena, 1742. *Note unusual spellings.*

[SELIG, GOTTFRIED] Der Jude, eine Wochenschrift. Erster Band [Also] Zweyter Band Erstes Stück[bis] Fünftes Stück. Leipzig, 1768.

[*Selig, Johann Friedrich Heinrich*] Johann Friedrich Heinrich Seligs, eines Bekehrten aus dem Judenthume, eigne Lebensbeschreibung. 2 volumes in 1. Leipzig, 1783.

[*Sonnenfels, Aloysius de*] WIENNER, ALOYSIUS, EDLER VON SONNENFELS [PERLIN LIPMANN] Aus denen Orientalischen Sprachen hergeholter Beweis der Wahrheit des Christ-Catholischen Schau-Brods, Oder Der Leiblichen Gegenwart Christi Im Abendmahl . . . Wien, 1753.

SONNENFELS [JOSEPH VON] La scienza del buon governo. Venezia, 1785.

TAIT, WALTER. The Conversion of God's Ancient People, a Proper Object of Christian Solicitude, and Ground of Christian Joy. A Sermon . . . Dundee, 1811. *Not in Roth.*

Très-humble supplique de cinq mille Juifs Polonois & Hongrois, qui désirent embrasser la Foi Catholique, Apostolique & Romaine, & recevoir le Baptême. Leopold [Lwow] 1759. *Szajkowski, 1471.*

CONVERTS AND CONVERSIONISM II, *from 1851*

BARON, DAVID. A Divine Forecast of Jewish History. London, no date.

BARON (MRS.) [DAVID] "Aus Dem Cheder." Pictures of Jewish Life. London, no date.

BASSIN, ELIESER. The Modern Hebrew, and the Hebrew Christian. London, 1882.

BEDA [pseudonym of DR. FRITZ LÖHNER] Getaufte und Baldgetaufte. Wien, etc., 1925.

C., W. C. Warum leiden die Juden? (Jerusalem) no date.

CANTERA BURGOS, FRANCISCO. El poeta Ruy Sánchez Cota (Rodrigo Cota) y su familia de judios conversos. Madrid, 1970.

CLAPHAM, J. W. Why do the Jews suffer? Kilmarnock, no date [about 1940]

COOPER, DAVID L. The God of Israel. Los Angeles, California, 1967.

COOPER, DAVID L. [Messiah: Collection of pamphlets] Los Angeles, California. *Various dates.*

DE LEW, LEWIS. Ben-Olie. Episodes from the Journal of an Israelite, Converted to Christianity. Baltimore, no date (1887)

DELITZSCH, FRANZ. Israel Pick. Bekännelse utur djupet af ett judiskt hjärta. Mariehamn, 1899. *On cover: Åbo, 1899.*

DÖNGES, E[MIL] Die Judenfrage. Frankfurt am Main, no date.

EINSPRUCH, HENRY (editor) Would I? Would You? Baltimore, Maryland, 1970.

FARBSTEIN, DAVID. Die Stellung des Judentums zum Proselytenwesen. Zürich, 1950.

FRANK, ARNOLD (editor) Zeugen aus Israel. Hamburg, no date.

FRIEDMANN, FRITZ. Was ich erlebte! Memoiren. 2 volumes. Berlin, 1909–1910.

GINSBURG, JOHANNES. Judentum oder Meschiachtum? Bratislava, 1927.

GINSBURG, SOLOMON L. A Wandering Jew in Brazil. An Autobiography. Nashville, Tennessee, 1922.

GINSBURG, SALOMÃO L. Um Judeu Errante no Brasil (Autobiografia) Rio de Janeiro, 1970.

[*Goldstern*] Israel Goldstern. Ein Bild aus der neuesten Judenmission. Barmen, 1877.

ISAY, RUDOLF. Aus meinem Leben. Weinheim/Bergstr., 1960.

KLYBER, ARTHUR B. This Jew. He's a Jew. Once a Jew . . . 3 volumes. Chicago, Illinois, 1973.

KOPFSTEIN, SIGMUND. Ein Glaubenszwist im Hause Königswarter. Wien, 1895.

KUNERT, KARL. Er führt mich. Aufzeichnungen aus dem Leben eines Christen aus Israel. Dinglingen (Baden) no date.

LEE, ROBERT G. If I were a Jew. Chicago, 1970.

LÉMANN, AUGUSTIN. Histoire complète de l'idée messianique chez le Peuple d'Israël. Lyon and Paris, 1909.

LÉMANN, AUGUSTIN. La Vierge et l'Emmanuel. Paris, 1904.

LEVINSOHN, ISAAC. The Story of My Wanderings in "The Land of My Fathers." London and Glasgow, 1903.

[*Libermann, Francis*] ALVES, HENRIQUE. O venerável Libermann. Lisboa, 1952.

[*Libermann, Francis*] LA PLACE (PADRE) Vida do veneravel Padre Francisco Libermann. Guimarães, 1892. *Title-page states "Tomo primeiro" but it is complete work.*

[*Loewe*] SCHROER, HERMANN (editor) Blut und Geld im Judentum. Dargestellt am jüdischen Recht (Schulchan aruch), übersetzt von Heinrich Georg F. Loewe sen., 1836. 2 volumes. München, 1937–1938.

MARITAIN, RAISSA. We have Been Friends Together. Memoirs. New York, etc., 1947.

[*Medici*] SZANCER, H. The Exotic Medici. Flushing, New York, 1964. *Xeroxed.*

[*Neander*] HÜTTMANN, HILDE. August Neander (David Mendel) in seiner Jugendentwicklung. Hamburg, 1936. *Dissertation.*

[*Neander*] SCHULZE, LUDWIG. August Neander. Ein Gedenkblatt für Israel und die Kirche. Leipzig, 1890.

OESTERREICHER, JOHN M. Racisme-Antisémitisme-Antichristianisme. Documents et critique. New York, 1943.

ORTIZ, ANTONIO DOMINGUEZ. Los Judeoconversos en España y América. Madrid, 1971.

[*Petri*] ESBO, AAGE. Israelsmissionaeren Efraim Philemon Petri. København, 1932. *Petri's name originally Efraim Esner Schereschewsky.*

RATISBONNE, MARIE-THÉODORE. Histoire de Saint Bernard et de son siècle. 2 volumes. Paris, 1864.

RATISBONNE, THÉODORE. Réponses aux questions d'un Israélite de notre temps. Paris and Bruxelles, 1878.

ROI, J. DE LE. Israel sonst, jetzt und einst. Berlin, 1880.

ROSENSTOCK-HUESSY, EUGEN. Dienst auf dem Planeten. Kurzweil und Langeweile im Dritten Jahrtausend. Stuttgart, etc., 1965.

ROSENSTOCK-HUESSY, EUGEN. Des Christen Zukunft oder Wir überholen die Moderne. München, 1955.

RUTHERFORD, J. F. Trost für die Juden. No place, 1925.

SAMTER, N[ATHAN]. Judentaufen im 19. Jahrhundert. Mit besonderer Berücksichtigung Preussens dargestellt. Breslau. 1895.

[*Samuel, Edward*] A Brief Memoir of the Conversion and Call to the Ministry, of Edward Samuel, by Birth and Education a Polish Jew . . . London, 1860.

SCHADÄUS, ELIAS. Judenmissions-Tractate. Leipzig, 1892.

SCHERADSKY, ABRAHAM. Blandt jødiske Flygtninge. Oplevelser i Israelsmissionens tjeneste. København, 1955.

SCHERADSKY, A. Jøder, jeg mødte. Billeder fra den danske Israelsmission. København, 1939.

SCHLAMM, VERA (as told to) BOB FRIEDMAN. Pursued. Glendale, California, 1972.

[*Schulz, Stephan*] Stephan Schulz, ein Verkündiger der frohen Botschaft an Israel. Basel, 1881.

SCHWOB, RENÉ. Moi, Juif. Livre posthume. Paris, 1928.

[*Sonnenfels, Josef von*] LUSTKANDL, W. Sonnenfels und Kudler. Rede auf Josef von Sonnenfels und Josef von Kudler . . . 1891 . . . Wien, 1891.

[*Sonnenfels, Josef von*] MÜLLER, WILIBALD. Josef von Sonnenfels. Biographische Studie aus dem Zeitalter der Aufklärung in Oesterreich. Wien, 1882.

[*Sonnenfels, Josef von*] OSTERLOH, KARL-HEINZ. Josef von Sonnenfels und die österreichische Reformbewegung im Zeitalter des aufgeklärten Absolutismus. Lübeck and Hamburg, 1970.

[*Sonnenfels, Josef von*] ROLLETT, HERMANN. Briefe von Sonnenfels. Wien, 1874.

[*Stein, Edith*] ALEXANDER, C. Der Fall Edith Stein. Flucht in die Chimäre. Frankfurt am Main, 1969.

[*Stein, Edith*] HERBSTRITH, WALTRAUD (TERESIA A MATRE DEI OCD) Edith Stein. Meitingen-Freising, 1972.

Weckstimmen zur Belebung und Förderung der Liebe zur Mission unter den Juden. Beiblatt zu "Saat auf Hoffnung." Nummer 1. Leipzig, no date.

WEIL, SIMONE. La connaissance surnaturelle (Paris) 1950.

WEIL, SIMONE. Écrits de Londres et dernières lettres. Paris, 1957.

WEIL, SIMONE. L'enracinement (Paris) 1949.

WEIL, SIMONE. La pesanteur et la grâce. Paris, 1948.

WEIL, SIMONE. Vorchristliche Schau. München-Planegg, 1959.

WEIL, SIMONE. Venise sauvée. Tragédie en trois actes (Paris) 1955.

[*Weil, Simone*] ANDERSON, DAVID. Simone Weil. London, 1971.

[*Weil, Simone*] HEIDSIECK, FRANÇOIS. Simone Weil. Paris, 1965.

WIENER, ALFRED H. My Way to Life. The Testimony of a Jewish Seeker for Truth. Toronto, 1972.

WOLFF, PAULUS. Saligheten är af Judarne. Min Lefnadsteckning samt Reseminnen från Missionsresor i Polen 1886–1887. Stockholm, 1891.

Ein Wort zur Judenfrage von einem ehemaligen Juden. Berlin, 1880.

NAZI JUDAICA I

L'Allemagne en lutte pour la victoire de la culture occidentale. La nouvelle Allemagne et les Juifs. Berlin [about 1934]

[*Bartels*] SCHLÖSSER, RAINER. Adolf Bartels, Wesen und Werk. Berlin, 1937. *In: Wille und Macht, Volume 5, Number 22.*

BERGMEISTER, KARL. Der jüdische Weltverschwörungsplan. Die Protokolle der Weisen von Zion vor dem Strafgerichte in Bern. Erfurt, 1937.

Aufsehenerregende Enthüllungen der "Times" über das jüdische Weltprogramm zur Versklavung der Völker unter die jüdische Weltherrschaft [Broadside] National-Sozialistische Deutsche Arbeiter-Partei, München. München (about 1920)

FAUST, GEORG. Sozial- und wirtschaftsgeschichtliche Beiträge zur Judenfrage in Deutschland vor der Emanzipation . . . Giessen, 1937. *Disssertation.*

FRANK, WALTER. Hofprediger Adolf Stoecker und die christlichsoziale Bewegung. Hamburg, 1935.

GRUBE, WALTER. Quellen zur Geschichte der Judenfrage in Württemberg. No place, no date. *Offprint.*

HOLZ, KARL (editor) Des Stürmer's Kampf. Der Kampf geht weiter (Nürnberg, 1937)

JANTZEN, WALTHER. Die Juden. Herausgegeben von der Antisemitischen Aktion. Heidelberg, etc., no date. *Second edition.*

JÜRGENS, JENS. Der Biblische Moses als Pulverfabrikant Räuberhauptmann und Erzbolschewist nach dem Zeugnis der Bibel. Eine Schlussabrechnung des Germanentums mit Moses, seinem Gott und dem A. Testament. Weissenburg in Bayern (1935)

LEERS, JOHANN VON. 14 Jahre Judenrepublik. Die Geschichte eines Rassenkampfes. 2 volumes (Berlin-Schöneberg, 1933)

[*Lueger*] SCHNEE, HEINRICH. Bürgermeister Karl Lueger. Leben und Wirken eines grossen Deutschen. Paderborn, 1936.

MATTHIESSEN, WILHELM. Israels Ritualmord an den Völkern. München, 1939.

RAABE, PETER. Die Musik im dritten Reich. Kulturpolitische Reden und Aufsätze. 1. Band. Regensburg, 1935.

[*Schönerer*] BIBL, VIKTOR. Georg von Schönerer. Ein Vorkämpfer des Grossdeutschen Reiches. Leipzig, 1942.

[*Schönerer*] MAYER-LÖWENSCHWERDT, ERWIN. Schönerer, der Vorkämpfer. Wien-Leipzig, 1938.

SCHROER, HERMANN (editor) Blut und Geld im Judentum. Dargestellt am jüdischen Recht (Schulchan aruch), übersetzt von Heinrich Georg F. Loewe sen., 1836. 2 volumes. München, 1937–1938.

SEITZ, HANNS, H. Kleines Juden-Brevier. Leipzig, 1939.

STEIN, FRANZ (editor) Hammer Jahrbuch für 1935–1938. 4 volumes. Wien (1934–1937)

VOGELSANG, ERICH. Luthers Kampf gegen die Juden. Tübingen, 1933.

Der Weltkampf. Monatsschrift für Weltpolitik völkische Kultur, und die Judenfrage in aller Welt. 16. Jahrgang, Heft 181. München, 1939.

ZIMMERMANN, HEINRICH. Staatsangehörigkeit und Reichsbürgerschaft unter besonderer Berücksichtigung des Judenproblems. Düsseldorf, 1940. *Dissertation.*

NAZI JUDAICA II

CRAEMER, RUDOLF. Benjamin Disraeli. Praha, 1943.

JACOBI, WALTER. Golem . . . Geissel der Tschechen. Die Zersetzung des tschechischen Nationalismus. Prag, 1942.

PREZIOSI, GIOVANNI. Come il giudaismo ha preparato la guerra. Roma, 1939–XVIII.

SERAPHIM, PETER-HEINZ. Il Giudaismo nell'Sud-Orientale. Roma, XIX–1941.

THOMAS-CHEVALLIER, HUBERT. La protection légale de la race. Essai sur les lois de Nuremberg. Paris, 1942.

On ADOLF HITLER

BLUME, BERNHARD. Hitler's Mein Kampf. Mills College, California, 1939.

JEWS UNDER THE NAZIS

BERTELSEN, AAGE. Oktober 43. Ereignisse und Erlebnisse während der Judenverfolgung in Dänemark. München, 1960.

HILL, MAVIS M. AND WILLIAMS, L. NORMAN. Auschwitz in England. A record of a libel action. London, 1965.

Judenlos unter Hitler. Die Ausrottung der Juden in Warschau und ihr Heldenhafter Widerstand. Schweiz, 1944.

MEIER, KURT. Kirche und Judentum. Die Haltung der evangelischen Kirche zur Judenpolitik des Dritten Reiches. Halle (Saale) 1968.

MOSER, JONNY. Die Judenverfolgung in Österreich 1938–1945. Wien, etc., 1966.

PRESSER, J. Ondergang. De vervolging en verdelging van het Nederlandse Jodendom 1940–1945. 2 volumes. 's-Gravenhage, 1965.

Stärker als die Angst. Den sechs Millionen, die keinen Retter fanden. Berlin, 1968.

WULF, JOSEPH. Musik im Dritten Reich. Eine Dokumentation. Gütersloh, 1963.

JUDAICA PUBLISHED UNDER THE NAZIS

Adressbuch für den Jüdischen Buchhandel. Berlin-Charlottenburg [1937]

Alijah. Informationen für Palästina Auswanderer. Berlin, 1935.

Almanach des Schocken Verlags auf das Jahr 5694. Berlin, 1933/34.

ARONSTEIN, PHILIPP (editor) Pictures of Jewish Life. From Israel Zangwill, Children of the Ghetto. Berlin, 1935.

BERKOVITS, ELI L. Was ist der Talmud. Berlin, 1938.

BÖHM, ADOLF. Die zionistische Bewegung 1918 bis 1925. Berlin, 1937.

BUBER, MARTIN. Die Frage an den Einzelnen. Berlin, 1936.

FRUMKIN, H. Krise in Palästina? Tatsachen und Perspektiven der Palästinawirtschaft auf Grund der Ergebnisse von 1932 bis 1935. Berlin, 1936.

Habinjan, Sammelschrift des Habonim. Berlin, 1936.

Haboneh. Sammelschrift des Habonim anlässlich seines fünfjährigen Bestehens. Berlin, 1938.

HEINE, HEINRICH. Der Rabbi von Bacherach. Berlin, 1937. *Wilhelm, I/547.*

HESCHEL, ABRAHAM. Maimonides. Eine Biographie. Berlin, 1935.

Das Jahr 1938. Kalender der Berliner Juden (Berlin, 1937)

Wo Juden bei Juden wohnen können . . . Berlin, 1937.

NOACK, FRITZ. Briuth. Gesundheitsratgeber für Palästina. Berlin, 1936.

PAPPENHEIM, BERTHA. Gebete (Berlin) 1936.

PICARD, JAKOB. Der Gezeichnete. Jüdische Geschichten aus einem Jahrhundert. Berlin, 1936.

POLLAK, ADOLF. Zionismus. Eine historische Darstellung . . . nebst einer Chronik. Berlin, 1934.

REIFENBERG, ADOLF. Denkmäler der jüdischen Antike. Berlin, 1937.

ROSENZWEIG, FRANZ. Kleinere Schriften. Berlin, 1937.

SCHLESINGER, ABRAHAM. Im Zeichen der Wiedergeburt. Jüdische Essays. Berlin, 1935.

STERN, MORITZ. Der Regensburger Judenprozess 1476–1480. Berlin [1935]

STILLSCHWEIG, KURT. Die Juden Osteuropas in den Minderheitenverträgen. Berlin, 1936.

SZULWAS, MOSES. Die Juden in Würzburg während des Mittelalters. Berlin, 1934.

ZOBEL, MORITZ. Das Jahr des Juden in Brauch und Liturgie Berlin, 1936.

ANTI-NAZI LITERATURE

BEIMLER, HANS. En el campo de asesinos de Dachau. Barcelona (1937)

BEIMLER, HANS. Four Weeks in the Hands of Hitler's Hell-Hounds. The Nazi Murder Camp of Dachau. New York, no date.

[*Beimler*] PERUCHO, ARTURO. Hans Beimler. Barcelona [1937]

KOFFLER, DOSIO. Die Deutsche Walpurgisnacht. Ein Spiel in 5 Szenen. London, 1941. *Wilhelm Sternfeld and Eva Tredemann, Deutsche Exil-Literatur 1933–1945, page 181.*